DATE DUE

JA 1 9 '93			
NO 4 '94			
JN 1 6 07			

DEMCO 38-296

THE ONE PLACE

THE ONE PLACE

A New Role for American Schools

The Young & Rubicam Foundation

St. Martin's Press

New York

Grateful acknowledgement is made for permission to reprint from the following: "Free To Teach" by Joe Nathan, Rev. ed. New York, Pilgrim Press 1991.

THE ONE PLACE

ISBN: 0-312-06430-6

First Edition: March 1991

10 9 8 7 6 5 4 3 2 1

CONTENTS

INTRODUCTION

IN SEPTEMBER OF 1988, we established an Education Group at Young & Rubicam. The Group was asked to act as if the education establishment in this country had approached us like a paying client in trouble because their service was no longer working as effectively as it needed to. As with all such clients, we used all of the agency's talents and resources to probe into and analyze the status of primary and secondary school education in the U.S.A. The objective was to define the problem and a path of reform.

The Group's findings, as you will read in the following pages, is a rethinking of the role of schools in the United States to meet the real needs of our children and our society today and in the future.

Why did we do this? Believe me, not out of arrogance, but rather because the problem is so serious and we had reason to believe we could make a contribution. Y&R has a long and unusually deep tradition of public service. The Advertising Council, the driving force behind much of the public service advertising in the U.S., was established in 1942 by our founder, Raymond Rubicam. Y&R has been deeply involved in its work ever since. From our earliest campaigns for U.S. War Bonds, through our advertising for the Peace Corps, to today's efforts for the United Negro College Fund, we have seen our advertising *work* and we have been proud of our contribution.

Basically, we are a company of people who are paid to understand people—to be sensitive to what motivates them, what makes them tick or not tick.

Thus began an arduous 18-month adventure as our team probed into the workings of inner city, rural and suburban schools, analyzed data and interviewed educators and children from all over the country.

The team not only investigated schools but also the education system's organic connection to society as a whole. The Director of the Education Group, Margaret Mark, put it this way: "It is impossible to study schools in isolation, because so many things impact children's development and their ability to learn. We have chosen to examine how a whole constellation of enforcers and influencers are affecting child development in America and have studied the role that formal schooling plays—and could play—within this broader context."

There were only two rules: No clients involved, therefore no bias. The project was totally underwritten by Y&R's employees, our only stockholders. We paid the team and their expenses and paid for people who replaced them on their regular assignments. Second, I didn't want the team to rush to any "quick" or superficial conclusions. I would give the venture a full two years if necessary.

"It is our great advantage," I told the team, "that we have no political ax to grind and we have no preconceived conclusions. No one knows we are doing this. We have no timetable. All we want are new ideas." In this, the team has exceeded my expectations. They have come back with a clear and objective idea of what is wrong and how to make it right.

A word about the team. Working with Ms. Mark has been an unusually dedicated group of professionals. A particular word should be said about one of them, Ms. Dorothy Ackerman. Y&R's commitment to excellence in communications and concerns about the world around it are reflected in people like Ms. Ackerman. Her record is outstanding. George Gallup, who organized the first agency Research Department, Y&R's, hired Dorothy in 1940. She has excelled in "understanding people" ever since and has been particularly gracious and energetic going about it. Dorothy provided a vibrant link to our original involvement in public service work.

The result has reinforced another ambition I had for this project. I hoped that it might show a new way for a private institution to intervene in public issues through the free and unqualified contribution of the its most valuable assets: people and their skills. You be the judge of our success by that measure.

Almost 20 years ago, a Y&R creative team created a powerful slogan, "A mind is a terrible thing to waste." It was meant to wake people up to the dreadful wasting of the gifts of black children, who had no opportunity to go to college. The theme is more valid today than ever. But the minds that are being wasted are those of children of every color. And there are millions more of them being wasted.

Our educational system is going under—not for lack of money or ideas but for lack of a central vision, a galvanizing idea about what is wrong and how to fix it.

We think this book presents that idea. After you read it, I implore you to get into the act. Unless people like you do, the United States is going to be dragged down by the furious undertow—the dangerous energy of unlearned, underdeveloped youth.

So now, please read what Margaret and Dorothy and our principal writer, H.G. Bissinger III; Carol Spranger and Wendy Yaross of our Consumer Insights Department; David May, a former teacher and member of our Account Management Department, and Mark Stroock, a consultant in our Corporate Relations Department, have discovered.

Alex Kroll
Chairman & C.E.O.
Young & Rubicam Inc.

ONE

IS IT UNSAFE TO BE A CHILD IN AMERICA?

AMERICAN CHILDREN ARE SUFFERING from the impact of forces so damaging that a recent *Congressional Report* concluded that it is unsafe to be a child in this country.

Substance abuse. Chronic poverty. Widespread divorce. Fatherless homes. Parents working until all hours to make ends meet.

These problems become manifest—dramatically so—in our schools, because they are the only place all American children pass through and are evaluated. School is the nation's "window" on the success or failure of our ability to support, nurture and, ultimately, develop our children.

Even though our education system is hardly flawless, the root of our catastrophic crisis does not lie within the schools alone. In fact, once in a while, by virtue of fate, luck or extraordinary concern, people within the schools rescue children and transform their lives.

But these rescues are often left to chance. Millions of children are not blessed by such encounters.

Tidy, piecemeal remedies to "the education problem" are often proposed. Computers in the classroom. More math and science. Back to basics. Standards and measurements. Accountability. Choice. Original literature instead of textbooks. School-based management. The list goes on.

Will a back-to-basics approach help rescue American children? Will it enable schools to do so? Is the answer a more stringent curriculum and more standardized tests? Are these the cure to our national schools crisis?

Consider the facts about what today's children experience outside of the classroom:

- Over one million children annually experience divorce.
- The proportion of children living in a single-parent household has doubled over the past 15 years. It is projected that three-fifths of today's children will spend at least part of their school years living with just one parent.
- Twenty percent of all American children and nearly half of all black children live in poverty.
- Only 27 percent of households with school-age children today consist of one working and one non-working parent.
- Four out of ten parents admit that their child is often alone after school has let out.

Dealing with these conditions—working with our children in school—presents this country with an entirely new set of social problems. For the first time in our history, the other institutions which once gave our children support are not there or are weakened. Community. Church. Extended family. Even the nuclear family.

As noted, we have used our skills and talents to examine these problems. The result is the analysis in this book and the recommendations with which we conclude. In the book we are not trying to lay guilt on any group that has attempted to deal with the education of children—teachers, parents, political organizations, the schools themselves. Rather, we have tried to discern root causes, to find solutions that have been discovered by many people in many sections of the country, and show how they can fit the needs of various communities and differing populations.

History and our own experiences have shown that nothing really changes in this country until its citizens want change to occur, and are willing to act on those wants and needs in their own lives. That is the goal of the research we have done and the solutions we present. We hope that the following chapters will help to increase awareness of the problems, stimulate citizens in all walks of life to see the need and, by their actions, cause change.

TWO

THE ONE PLACE

LORRAINE MONROE HAS A dream.

In her mind's eye she can see it perfectly—a kind of place that should exist in this country but doesn't—one that is every bit as vital to the community as the church once was or the cozy village square or the parish, a place that is open 18 hours a day and isn't just for the kids who are assigned to go there but also for their brothers and sisters and mothers and fathers.

"A one-stop shop" is how Lorraine Monroe likes to describe it, a place where kids know from the very first moment they step inside that something wonderful and exciting is about to happen—"a magic carpet ride to the rest of your life."

It would be a place of nurturing, but a place of high expectation. It would be a place of demand, but a place where a child always felt a sense of warmth and belonging and connection. It would be a place to learn about reading, but also a place to learn about life.

What would something like that possibly be called? Lorraine Monroe has a simple answer: a school.

That's right. A *school*.

Her dream isn't some pie-in-the-sky fantasy plucked out of the air. It isn't based upon wishful thinking, or wanting to be the latest person to throw her hat into the ring and join the ever-popular crusade of how to fix our country's deeply troubled school system.

Her vision is based upon the experience of being a teacher, principal and administrator in the New York City school system. It is based upon being a former Director of Bank Street College Center for Minority Achievement. It is based upon a deep and abiding love and respect for children and knowing that *all* kids, regardless of skin color and background, can learn and blossom under the right conditions.

As far as Lorraine Monroe is concerned, the answer to the crisis doesn't lie in teacher-bashing. It doesn't lie in increasing the number of standardized tests. It doesn't lie in trying to run schools in the same way that you run a business, using competitive models and financial incentives. The answer isn't freedom of choice, or tuition vouchers, or a national curriculum, or all the other things you read about almost daily in the newspaper. To Lorraine Monroe, these are stop-gap measures that will not have any lasting impact.

Instead the answer lies with reinventing the definition of a school and making it the one consistent institution in a child's life—the place that *guarantees* that children receive the physical and emotional support that is essential to their learning and developing. "If we don't start doing some things differently, if we don't train people and give them the autonomy they need, I don't want to think about what could happen," says Lorraine Monroe. "I don't think we have a whole lot of time."

* * *

When Yale child psychiatrist James Comer became involved in two elementary schools in New Haven, Connecticut, in 1968, there was skepticism and resistance, not to mention a general sense of hopelessness. The two schools, Simeon Baldwin and Martin Luther King Jr., had the lowest achievement records of any elementary schools in the city. Attendance was poor, staff morale was low and parents were angry and distrustful.

It was a situation that had already caused many to give up. But Comer, Director of the School Development Program at the Yale Child Study Center, felt he had a way of reversing the failure cycle.

The kids who went to these schools, he was convinced, were not inherently bad despite their frequent behavioral problems. They weren't incapable of learning or acting properly in the classroom. The basic problem, he felt, was that they were socially and psychologically underdeveloped because of a society that no longer provided any anchors.

Comer was convinced that if you could create a school where emphasis on academics went hand in hand with emphasis on child development, you would create an atmosphere in which learning would thrive.

That was the theory.

Then came the reality. He walked into a classroom at Simeon Baldwin on that first day and found two 8-year-olds chasing each other. Two others were standing on tables screaming. Several others were crying, "Teacher, teacher." Comer called for order, which seemed almost laughable. They ignored him and he retired to the hallway.

"One part of me said, 'What am I doing here?' and wanted to run. The other part of me said, 'You want to make a difference—and this is your chance.' "

Comer stayed and began to implement the changes that he felt would be the key to educational success in a setting where there never had been any success at all.

He established a governance and management team at each school made up of trained parents, teachers, administrators and support staff. Together the team identified the most pressing problems facing the school and developed specific plans for improvement. He established a mental health team to apply child development knowledge to almost every phase of school life. The emphasis was on keeping abreast of the development of each student, and trying to head off problems before they evolved into major crises.

Change came slowly and there were numerous occasions in which it was hard to see evidence of any progress. One of the schools, Baldwin, opted out of the program. But the work continued at King. Initial distrust over Comer's methods drifted away and a sense of trust developed between teachers, students and parents. Outbursts inside the classroom became less and less frequent. But to make the program a true success, Comer knew he needed quantifiable proof. It happened in the late seventies when the results of the Iowa Test of Basic Skills were released. The scores at King had improved markedly.

"When I saw the results in math and reading, the two areas we had targeted for improvement, I jumped for joy and danced around the office," Comer wrote. At last, after nearly ten years of work, he had the ammunition he needed to show that his ideas had merit.

In the late sixties, when the battle to improve King truly did seem futile, the achievement scores at the school ranked the second worst in the district. In recent years the scores of fourth-graders there have ranked the third highest of the 26 elementary schools in the district.

To Comer, the reason for that success is hardly

mysterious. Most American schools, he feels, instead of helping a child develop, do just the opposite. Instead of school becoming the one place where children know they belong, it becomes just another place to which they feel no meaningful connection. The result of that alienation is all too obvious—anger, outbursts, dropping out.

But it doesn't have to be that way. School, instead of simply adding to the instability of a child's life, can become the very core of it.

Structured the right way, Comer says, school can still give children "what they need to make it in the mainstream of society." The institutions that once supported children—family, community and church—have deteriorated so badly, he feels, that school is our last hope. "School's the only place we have in this society," says Comer flatly. "There is no other place."

* * *

It was obvious to Ted Sizer that something was fundamentally wrong.

Three years of traveling around the country from high school to high school gave Sizer, the former Dean of Harvard Graduate School of Education and former Headmaster of Phillips Academy, a keen insight into what was happening in the nation's classrooms.

What he discovered was a deep and fundamental crisis, a way of teaching that was outdated and out-moded, guided by bells that rang every 55 minutes, and constant interruptions for announcements over a scratchy public address system that sounded like a high-pitched whine.

The classroom wasn't a place of high energy. It wasn't a place of high expectation. It was a virtual dead zone. To Sizer, the problem was obvious: High school classrooms, the way they were structured, were getting in the way of learning. There was no one-on-one. There was no give and take. The teacher stood at the front of the room and lectured in a monotone drone. The students, feeling no responsi-bility to learn for themselves, jotted down notes and became quickly adept at figuring out what they needed to know to squeeze through the exam. To Sizer it was a crisis situation.

"We must get away from the 'donation' metaphor of education in which teachers give and students receive," says Sizer. "People learn by being involved, by doing things for themselves. I want a new meta-phor—the student as worker to whom teachers turn over the main task of learning."

It was a wonderful statement, the kind of thing you would expect to hear from someone who had spent much of his academic career running one of the most prestigious prep schools in the country. But on a practical level, did it mean anything at all? Could the entrenched relationship between teacher and student be turned topsy-turvy and completely reinvented?

Sizer has tried exactly that with something called the Coalition of Essential Schools.

Today there are about 50 such schools in 19 states, adhering in one way or another to the Sizer creed. Instead of being at the mercy of the school bell, many classes at these schools go on for two hours at a time. Instead of breaking up the day into compartmentalized subjects, there is an emphasis on bringing different subjects together in the classroom, to show how history, English and science are interrelated.

The emphasis is no longer on regurgitation and the taking of tests. Instead, through the assigning of projects in which there are few carefully prescribed rules, much of the responsibility for learning, and figuring out conclusions, is placed where it should be—on the shoulders of the student.

There is evidence that students placed in Coalition of Essential School programs have better attendance rates than their counterparts in regular school. There is also evidence of better academic performance. But the most telling aspect of the program is the reaction of the students. They talk about being challenged, engaged, pushed, even pressured to think, learn and take charge of their own education.

In an affluent suburb of New York City, Coalition students described their class:

"It's hard, but it's fun."

"There's more discussion; we're not note-takers. We really don't have to take a lot of notes to learn. Because we talk about things, we're able to understand more."

In East Harlem, students said:

"You can't hide out the way you can in a regular classroom. You don't fall between the cracks. You're involved."

"What you learn makes more sense."

And in middle-class Manitowoc, Wisconsin, a sophomore lamented the persistent—and unfamiliar—pressure to *think*:

"That's what it's been like all year. There's no break from it."

Monroe. Comer. Sizer.

Their ideas about education are innovative and different, but none of them is utopian. The very thing that separates them from other reform advocates may be the very depth of their realism. They have come to grips with the educational crisis in America, and they innately understand that the only way to solve the crisis of the American school is to completely reshape it.

While their approaches vary somewhat, the fundamental principles underlying their solutions are the same—high *expectations* for real learning and the guarantee of individualized *support* that makes that possible.

As Ted Sizer puts it, "No two good schools are alike, but all good schools are informed by the same ideas."

Schools are being expected to do more than they have at any point in the nation's history. And yet the very foundation of the environment in which schools operate has been dramatically transformed.

"The children in our community have no place to go," says a teacher from a public elementary school in a socioeconomically mixed neighborhood. "There's no church. There's no athletic group. The playgrounds don't want them. Their families don't want them."

"The burden is nurturing," says another teacher from the same school. "I could become mom to three-quarters of my class. But I have my own children."

Where can a child go to feel wanted? Where can a child go to belong and feel part of a community? To become engaged in something that will develop his sense of self and his sense of worth?

For Monroe, it is the concept of school as the one-stop shop, an all-day, all-night gas station that offers so many things it becomes vital to every family member. For Comer, it is the concept that schools must teach the whole person. For Sizer, it is a fundamental change in the relationship between teacher and student that will make the classroom a place for real learning and not just mindless memorization.

School, in short, has to become the place that guarantees that children get what they need—nurturing, guidance, development, the ability to learn.

But it isn't a crisis of schools that is causing the school crisis.

It is a crisis of society.

To truly understand what is at stake, and also to understand what a school can become, listen to the words of Lorraine Monroe:

"For many kids across this country of lots of ethnic backgrounds, the school is the most predictable, consistent institution in their lives. Church is not there for kids anymore. Not even family for so many kids because of the growth of single-parent families.

"School must (and some teachers are really chafing at this) be *the* institution in the lives of children. It is the institution of change and transformation. It's got to do more than give the academic product.

"It's got to be a place where you learn to be a social human being. It's got to be the place where you start to figure out those things that you do and you don't do. It's got to be the place where you test your competency, where you have people who care for you, where you eat breakfast, lunch and maybe in some places dinner.

"It becomes the safety net. It becomes the fail-safe place."

THREE

WHAT HAPPENED

THE SCHOOL, IN A large city in the northeastern corridor, is on the third floor above a hospital. It has been dubbed "St. Somewhere." To find directions to it, you talk to a policewoman who sits at a desk. It is a junior high for kids who have been placed here by the Committee on Special Education, and it is their last chance, their last hope. Some are violent. Some are pregnant.

"Wally," the school's crisis intervention teacher, pulls out a cardboard box filled with weapons he has taken from the kids, who range in age from 11 to 15. He pulls out a pair of brass knuckles with a secret built-in knife that pops out at the touch of a button. He pulls out an ice pick with a point that has been finely honed. He pulls out a kitchen knife with a deeply serrated edge.

"Wally" is a kind of miracle worker to these kids. He doesn't fear them. He doesn't find them hopeless. He sees and feels their potential, but he also knows the environment from which they come, a world of single mothers and crack and generational cycles of poverty.

"Wally" and the other people who work here do what they can to make school a safe, stable environment. They feed the kids breakfast at eight in the morning, bringing up trays of food from the kitchen. Despite the enormous odds against them, the teachers and administrators here do many things right. The teacher-to-student ratio, two staff members for every ten students, is conducive to real learning. Despite the bleak setting, despite the open despair, the school works. It succeeds.

And then comes the 3 p.m. bell.

With school over for the day, teachers personally escort the kids to the subway and put a token in the turnstile to try to make sure they get home. They give them one for the return trip in the morning to try to make sure they come back to school.

"We give these kids everything we can," says "Wally." "We make them breakfast. We give 'em a shower if they need it. I've seen teachers take money out of their own pockets to buy a kid clothes."

Given the kinds of conditions they labor under, it is hard not to feel as if some miracle is taking place here. Through hard work and devotion, they do create a sense of "family" for these kids, a sense of connecting, of belonging somewhere. The kind of behavior that is the norm in their outside lives—drugs, weapons, profanity, anger, lashing out without restraint—is not tolerated here. It is screened out, kept away. But the insulation only lasts seven hours a day, five days a week. What happens after that?

"It takes a long time to break through to one of our kids," says an administrator. "Sometimes you begin to see some progress. Then the kid leaves on Friday, friendly and cooperative, and comes back on Monday ready to tear the place apart. You have to think, God only knows what that kid went through over the weekend. You wouldn't believe what goes on in these kids' lives. Unspeakable things."

Will a back-to-basics approach help this school? Is the answer a more stringent curriculum and more standardized tests? Are those things the cure to the school crisis?

Listen to what the school's principal has to say:

"The business community is totally insensitive to what the schools are up against. Everyone imagines the period during which they went to school, oblivious to everything that has changed since then. Their proposals for reform assume life in the 1950s, or earlier.

"There are people in education right now who are heroes, who do spectacular things in spite of insurmountable odds. We know who they are, they're legendary to us.

"But no one outside of the schools would so much as recognize their names. What we're doing here in these schools is invisible to the rest of society."

"What's the key to breaking through to these kids?" the principal is asked.

"Being firm," he says. "Being fair." And then there is a pause before he names the last, most essential, ingredient.

"Being there."

* * *

In the 1940s, according to the California Department of Education, public school students in the United States claimed they faced these problems in school:

1. Talking
2. Chewing gum
3. Making noise
4. Running in the halls
5. Getting out of turn in line
6. Wearing improper clothing
7. Not putting paper in wastebaskets

In the 1980s, the list had changed as follows:

1. Drug abuse
2. Alcohol abuse
3. Pregnancy
4. Suicide
5. Rape
6. Robbery
7. Assault

The proof is everywhere that American schools are serving a population with needs that never could have been imagined 30 or 40 years ago. The impact of that has been enormous.

The 1989 edition of the *Digest of Education Statistics*, published by the Office of Educational Research and Improvement of the U.S. Department of Education, is not the kind of title that seems destined for the best-seller list. It contains charts and graphs, about 400 pages of them, and it doesn't take long for the tiny type to become numbing.

But the *Digest of Education Statistics* tells a gripping story, and in those tiny columns of tiny numbers lies the saga of American education—the fantastic scope of what it has tried to do, what it has accomplished and how it has dismally failed in comparison to other countries around the world.

From *Digest*, Table 8, p. 15: In 1940, among those 25 and over in the United States, 24 percent had at least four years of high school. In 1988, the figure had jumped to 76 percent. Among whites, the figure rose from 26 percent to 78 percent. Among blacks and other races, it jumped from eight percent to 67 percent.

This means that over the past 50 years, the country has dramatically shifted from an era in which only a select few were educated to an era in which virtually every American, regardless of race or socioeconomic background, has the opportunity to get an education.

When people talk nostalgically about the good old days of the forties and fifties, when they wonder why the school of today can't be as wholesome and trouble-free as the school of yesterday, when they shake their heads at the "St. Somewheres," they may not realize that the American educational system back then was only available to those squarely within the mainstream. Minorities were basically excluded. So were the poor. But that has changed.

In 1939–40, total enrollment in educational institutions (not including college) was 29.5 million. In the fall of 1990, that figure was estimated to be 59.3 million, more than double.

That figure is good news, for it reflects that the American mandate to educate all children is a strong and serious one. It also means that education in America is not used as a screening tool to weed out the weak from the strong. It is a wonderful accomplishment, one the country should be proud of, the very essence of democracy—but it has not come easily.

"Remember, in the 1950s we were graduating only a little over 50 percent of all children who started school in the United States," wrote LeRoy Hay, a former National Teacher of the Year. "Today that figure is over 75 percent. Who are the additional 25 percent? They are the kids we used to drop by the wayside, kids with problems and special needs."

What are some of those problems?

From *Digest*, Table 17, p. 23: In 1970, there were 5.5 million single-parent families in which the father was not present. In 1988 that figure had almost doubled to 10.6 million. That is extremely unsettling news, for teachers everywhere will tell you that the single biggest impact on a child's self-esteem is his or her home life. And studies have consistently shown that parental involvement, particularly the *father's* involvement, is highly correlated with academic achievement.

Are schools financially equipped to handle the social needs of today's student?

From *Digest*, Table 25, p. 29: The percentage of GNP spent on public education has decreased over the past 15 years, from a high of 7.4 percent in 1974 to 6.9 percent in 1989.

Are teachers emotionally equipped to handle the social needs of today's student? What is their morale like?

From *Digest*, Table 59, p. 72: In 1966, 53 percent of those polled by the National Education Association said they would "certainly" teach again. In 1976, 37 percent said they would "certainly" teach again. In 1986 the figure had dropped to 23 percent.

In 1966, only two percent said they would "certainly" not teach again. Twenty years later nine percent said they would definitely not do it.

Given what teachers feel about education today, what about parents?

From *Digest*, Table 22, p. 27: In a poll taken for

Metropolitan Life by Louis Harris & Associates, only 12 percent of those parents polled felt that school systems did an "excellent" job of preparing their children for jobs after high school. When asked to assess the degree to which students seemed motivated to learn, only 15 percent of those parents polled rated it as "excellent."

What is the upshot of all these factors? How are America's students performing?

From *Digest*, Table 343, p. 388: In an international assessment of mathematics proficiency for 13-year-olds that was conducted in 1988, the United States ranked the worst of the 12 countries and provinces that participated, worse than Ireland, worse than Ontario, worse than the United Kingdom, worse than Spain. The United States' score of 474 was 36 points lower than the score from the next lowest country, the United Kingdom.

From *Digest*, Table 347, p. 390: In a survey of science scores for 17 countries from 1983 to 1986, the United States scored in the middle of the pack among 10-year-olds. Among 14-year-olds, only the Philippines and Hong Kong did worse. Poland, Hungary, Italy, and Australia, among others, all had higher scores.

From *Digest*, Table 348, p. 391: In a survey of science scores for 12th graders from 13 countries, the United States scored the worst in biology, the third worst in chemistry, and the fifth worst in physics.

Statistics can be misleading. They can be used to generate a host of conclusions, some true, some faulty. But the evidence here seems clear that the American education system, however noble in its mission of teaching all students, really isn't teaching them much at all. When compared with Japan—or even Poland or Italy or Canada—the U.S. results are embarrassing.

By now, the news of these statistics is hardly shattering. Americans have been worrying about their educational system for almost a decade, their concerns prompted by a devastating report that was issued in 1983 by the National Commission on Excellence in Education called "A Nation at Risk." The Commission painted an almost frightening picture of American education:

"... the educational foundations of our society are presently being eroded by a rising tide of mediocrity that threatens our very future as a nation and a people. What was unimaginable a generation ago has begun to occur—others are matching and surpassing our educational attainments.

"If an unfriendly foreign power had attempted to impose on America the mediocre educational performance that exists today, we might well have viewed it as an act of war. As it stands, we have allowed this to happen to ourselves. We have squandered the gains in student achivement made in the wake of the Sputnik challenge. Moreover, we have dismantled essential support systems which helped make those gains possible. We have, in effect, been committing an act of unthinking, unilateral educational disarmament."

To back up that sweeping conclusion, the Commission noted that nearly 40 percent of high school seniors could not draw inferences from written material; only one-fifth could write a persuasive essay, and only one-third could solve a mathematics problem requiring several steps. The Commission also noted a steady decline in Scholastic Aptitude Tests (SAT) and achievement scores.

The conclusions reached by the Commission were shocking, and they came as a rude awakening to a nation that had always prided itself on its educational preeminence.

What happened?

How is it that a school system that was once regarded as the world's finest became one of the world's worst?

The National Commission on Excellence pointed to a weakened curriculum in which students had been allowed to steer away from college preparatory and vocational courses. The Commission also concluded that expectations placed upon the students were abysmally low. Two-thirds of high school seniors reported less than one hour of homework a night. The Commission also noted the puzzling paradox in which students' average grades continued to rise while achievement scores continued to plummet.

Coupled with a lack of homework, the Commission also noted that American students simply did not spend enough time in school. In American high schools, the report said, the typical day lasted six hours and the typical school year was about 180 days. In England and other industrialized countries, according to the report, the average school day was eight hours and the typical school year was 220 days.

In its recommendations, the Commission advocated a return-to-basics approach. It called for a strengthened curriculum that would include four years of English in high school, three years of mathematics, three years of science, three years of social studies and a half-year of computer science.

"We recommend that schools, colleges and universities adopt more rigorous and measurable standards, and higher expectations, for academic performance and student conduct, and that four-year colleges and universities raise their requirements for admission," said the report. "This will help students do their best educationally with challenging materials in an environment that supports learning and authentic accomplishment."

The Commission's recommendations did not fall on deaf ears. Bolster the curriculum, many reasoned, push students to do more with rigorous testing, and the problems of the schools will be solved and there won't be a crisis anymore.

But is that the case?

In New Jersey, Governor Jim Florio announced that the state would be scaling back its school testing program after determining that it was having the opposite effect of what had originally been intended. Teachers, under enormous pressure for students to do well, were spending valuable time "teaching the test." Students, in turn, were simply being inundated with facts that would enable them to perform well on these tests but did not result in much learning. The National Assessment of Educational Progress, the study that systematically attempts to monitor what American children know, showed a small increase in math and reading scores on the national level, perhaps reflective of the back-to-basics movement. But at the same time, students seemed increasingly incapable of reasoning for themselves.

On balance, it is hard to see how the back-to-basics push could revolutionize the schools.

At the same time, it seemed that money alone is not the solution:

"If increased spending on education offered a way out of the problems, everyone would no doubt favor the spending; there are few items on the national agenda more important," noted *Forbes* in 1990. "But the problems of the U.S. education industry, like those of the Soviet economy, are structural.

"In both cases, the problems cannot be resolved by mere tinkering reforms or more spending. You don't fix a car that isn't running properly by pumping gasoline into the tank."

A fix for the schools has proved so elusive because so many of those actively trying to solve the problem, however earnest and well-intended, don't seem to understand the true cause of it.

A veritable social revolution has dramatically altered the environment for child rearing and education. The student of today, regardless of his or her socioeconomic background, is not like the student of yesterday. But many business leaders and government leaders, groping for answers, tend to dismiss the effect of these changes on American education. As the principal from "St. Somewhere" puts it, "Their proposals for reform assume life in the 1950s, or earlier."

Certainly, a school like "St. Somewhere," designed for troubled children, is going to see a hideous host of social problems. But our research clearly indicates that virtually every school in America encounters social problems that have a direct impact on children's ability to learn. And very few schools are equipped to deal with this.

Our highest-performing students tend to compare favorably with students anywhere else on the globe, including Japan. They tend to be the children of parents who are highly educated themselves, parents who place a very high value on education and are actively involved in their children's development.

But even among this elite group, problems are increasingly evident.

"If you gave me a million dollars to build programs to rectify the impact divorce has had on *one* kid's development," a principal in a super-affluent community remarked, "I'm not sure I could do it."

For these children, extraordinary, sometimes excessive "performance" expectations—measured by SAT scores and admission to elite schools and colleges—are increasingly unaccompanied by the essential emotional support. Some kids fall victim to anxiety and depression. Others devise very sophisticated strategies to "work the system"—ace the test, get into the right schools, land the job—often in collusion with parents and teachers who share the same priorities.

A growing number of educators are calling attention to what they've labeled a "silent conspiracy" or "unholy pact" to circumvent real *learning* among these most privileged young people and adults.

Even so, the most dramatic and disturbing evidence of social change is among children from middle-class homes and from the growing ranks of the disadvantaged.

In communities that could still appear in a Norman Rockwell poster, concerned teachers are encountering the frightening impact of change.

Here's how one elementary school teacher expressed sentiments that were repeated again and again:

"The children don't have the emotional support that they at one time did have. We expect a lot more of them. We expect them to be older than they really are. They come home—there's no one home. They have a lot of responsibilities. They have no one really to talk to. I think that over the years I find that I end up talking more to my students about everyday happenings in their lives, and trying to help them meet their disappointments, than I ever did, because they have no one to turn to.

"It's not that their parents don't care. It's just that the parents are busy. They're busy trying to make a living for these children. It gets harder and harder for these parents. And we have a lot of single, sole-support families where the mother has to work until 5:00 or 6:00 o'clock. And it's very difficult for these children. We expect a lot of them."

And this is how one caring principal represented a common concern about incoming first-graders:

"They seem to be coming in with less and less of an ability to sit still or pay attention. More and more impairments of one kind or another. I don't know the reasons. And as much as I like TV for its good points, I sure don't like it for what it's doing for our kids in terms of paying attention.

"They watch cartoons and then the 30-second commercial comes in bombarding them with so many messages in 30 seconds, and then out again. Then back to cartoons, moving fast with music in the background and people socking each other, and then into the commercial again. It's inhuman. It's an inhuman pace. An inhuman thing to do to kids.

"I don't know how many of them on a summer day sit under a tree and read a book anymore. I would suspect very few."

Among these children of the middle class, there is this reluctant, but growing neglect. It is caused by divorce, and also by the intense economic pressures placed on parents to work as many hours as it takes to hold on to the American dream of house and car and material pleasures. And it is exacerbated by the growing transience and impermanence of a society in which one-fifth of all American families move every year, and in which caring grandparents, aunts, uncles, neighbors and clergymen are increasingly absent from children's daily lives.

However emotionally needy they are, these middle-class children tend to eventually fit comfortably into the culture of the school; in fact, they tend to fade right into the woodwork.

Not so in our inner city schools.

Among many disadvantaged children the problems are so enormous, and the cultural gap between school and home so wide, that the classroom is another reflection of the chaos in children's lives. Attention disorders, problems of relating and acting out are often evident from the first day of school. For many, the culture of the school is unfamiliar and intimidating, the developmental demands of learning in a group setting are unachievable.

Millions of these children disengage or drop out long before the "stay in school" slogans ever reach their ears.

How did this happen? How did the situation get this bad?

Prior to 1940, James Comer wrote in his book, "School Power," "The school, the principal and the staff were an intimate and highly respected part of the social networks of most families. Their authority was an extension of parental authority. Even the school building was hallowed ground.

"In towns of yesterday, tight-knit networks of people, in general agreement about what was right and wrong, significantly shaped the development and behavior of children."

Mobility added to the fragmentation of life. After World War II, families began to uproot themselves in record numbers. The school teacher was inclined to move as well, often to a community far away from the one in which he or she taught. Instead of being a fixture in the community, someone with whom you did your shopping and went to church, the teacher became a stranger. Opportunities for natural, day-to-day contact were eliminated. (It is now estimated that 77 percent of all Americans live in major metropolitan areas, and that 18 percent of all American families move each year.)

In the post-World War II era, the familiar lines of authority broke down as well. It wasn't just the minister and the parent and the school teacher exposing children to ideas; it was everyone, through radio and television.

The impact of television cannot be underestimated. The advent of cable television, where a child now typically has as many as 50 different channels to choose from at any given moment, has only heightened that influence. Research shows that babies 2 and under watch an average of two hours of television a day and children 2 to 5 watch four hours a day. By fourth grade one-third of all children watch six hours or more of television a day.

By the time a student graduates from high school, according to research by Yale University professor Victor Strasburger, he or she has spent 15,000 hours camped in front of a television set during which they have witnessed 18,000 murders and 350,000 commercial messages.

"No longer are a few local leaders the holders of all truth," James Comer wrote. "The common tongue or general agreement among local authority figures about what is right and wrong no longer exists. It is possible to hear differences of opinion expressed about the most basic issues—for example, what constitutes freedom of choice, life, death—almost every half-hour on radio and television newscasts."

Television, mass transportation, the lack of clearly

defined authority figures, the unraveling of the family and community—all these influences have resulted in a dangerous sense of alienation. With increasing futility and frustration, young children are trying to respond to a world that offers inadequate emotional, psychological and social support systems.

Because of the drastic changes in society, a dangerous paradox has developed. On the one hand, children, because of all the influences of mass communication, seem "worldly" beyond their years. But many of them have nothing to ground them. They seem independent and outgoing, and yet behind that confident facade is an acute anxiousness and loneliness. They seem committed to the practical value of schooling. They presumably understand why it is important. But they also seem uncertain how anything they learn in school relates to their lives. What good is history? What good is reading? What good is anything? To teachers, children seem to have no moral center. Says the principal of an elementary school in New Jersey:

> ". . . some of them will come into the office and I will say, 'Don't you know that what you did was wrong? Doesn't it bother you that somebody else was offended by what you did?' [There is] no registering as to whether I am getting through or not. Now there are only a couple of those like that in here. But it looks like some of them have no conscience. They are growing up without a conscience for right or wrong.

They're the ones that scare you. They just don't care."

The experience of that principal is not uncommon. If all a school administrator had to do was ease the process of actual teaching, there would probably be no education crisis. But administrators, whether in New York or New Jersey, Wisconsin or Minnesota, don't have that luxury.

St. Paul, Minnesota, is not a city known for problems. In fact it is a city known for just the opposite, having a reputation for being clean, safe and friendly. But the typical school day of school administrator Joe Nathan, as described in his book, "Free To Teach," clearly shows the impact that a changing society is having on the schools:

> 7:30–7:45: Conference with two parents and their daughters. The two 13-year-olds had a nasty fight the previous day . . . the girls had torn hair, scratched, and called each other names ranging from "whore" to "shit-eating nigger."
>
> The grandmother of one of the girls was angrier with me than she appeared to be with her granddaughter. She disagreed vehemently with my sending both girls home for the rest of the day . . .
>
> Convinced the girls were ready to return to class, I readmitted them. As the grandmother left the office, she muttered that I was a "honky bastard" just loudly enough for several nearby students to hear.
>
> 7:50: Took a phone call from a parent complaining

that I had forced her son to pay five dollars for a window broken as a result of a scuffle involving him and several other students. Her son clearly had not delivered the letter I'd given him to take home explaining the situation.

8:00–9:30: Our Pupil Problems Committee, which all St. Paul public schools have, met with a student, who had called in a false bomb scare, and his father.

The father's response to [the options presented] was that he had three older children in various penal institutions, he was fed up with his son, had beaten him and taken away all his privileges at home for the next month, and that we could do whatever we wanted to do . . . the father said he didn't want his son at home; he felt the best action would be to send the student to his grandparents' home in Iowa.

The meeting, which I feared would be both bitter and nasty, ended amiably, with the student thanking various staff members for helping him through the two years he'd been at our school. He told us that this was the best school among the nine he had attended. He was 13 years old.

9:30–10:30: Another conference . . . the two students were half brother and sister. Until the previous week, we thought they both had the same parents. We learned that the young woman had run away from home and gone to live with her sister. Her uncle (who we mistakenly thought was her father) came into the school to bring her home. The young woman begged us not to let her uncle take her away from the school . . . she claimed that her uncle abused her, and she wanted to leave his home. Under state law, school officials are required to report child abuse to the welfare department and police if it appears the claim is justified.

The girl's half brother learned somehow that she had filed a complaint. He began swearing and screaming at her, and she returned his comments in full. I'd stepped between them to prevent the boy from striking his sister and told him to go home for the rest of the day. He and I walked to the door together and I urged him to go directly home to cool off. Fifteen minutes later he was back in school with a two-by-four board several feet long!

10:45–11:00: Several students were just arriving for the day . . . they all said they liked their morning classes and did well when they attended them. However, they also liked staying up later and watching movies and television.

11:00–11:30: A teacher sent in two students who had been fighting. One was a boy with whom I'd had no previous contact, the other a youngster who constantly had problems. . . . One had called the other a "muscle-bound dummy," and the other retorted with "drug-running burnout." Both had challenged each other to "do something about it," which immediately produced flying punches.

12:32: Exactly eight minutes after I arrived in the faculty room, the public address speaker summoned me back to the office. "Is Joe there?"

"Yes."

"Please come to the office immediately."

On my way to the office I encountered a teacher so angry she didn't want to wait until I got back. "Six or seven little monsters just picked up my car and tried to move it. I have no idea how much damage was done."

3:30–4:30: Wrote letters to or phoned several parents about problems or progress. One conversation went something like this:

"Hello, Mr. Taylor? This is Joe Nathan from Murray Junior High. How are you this afternoon?"

"What's that damn son of mine done now? Lord, we just talked a week ago."

"That's why I'm calling—to tell you that whatever you said to him really worked. His conduct in science class has improved dramatically. He's bringing his materials to class, and the teacher reports that he's turned in several back assignments. She also says he is raising his hand when he wants to say something. We're really pleased and wanted to share that progress with you!"

"Say what? Hey, who is this really?"

I assured him that he was talking with his son's assistant principal.

"Do you know that this is the first time anyone from a school has ever called to say something good about my son? Thanks, thanks a lot, man."

Given the kinds of conditions that school teachers and administrators labor under, the depth of their dedication seems almost miraculous. It is unfair to hold them responsible for the failure of our educational system.

What the system hasn't done is adapt to the massive social changes that have taken place and figure out a way to make school an essential part of a child's life.

"There has been very little or no change in school

structure and management to accommodate these massive technological, social and relationship changes and needs," Comer wrote. "The response of educators has been to develop largely technological solutions—new math, new machines, new buildings, new curricula—for what are essentially personal development, interpersonal and inter-group problems."

FOUR

WHAT DIDN'T HAPPEN

To GET A SENSE of what goes on in a classroom today, it isn't necessary to go to the bookstore and buy one of the dozens of books that have come out in recent years about the deteriorating state of education.

To get a look at the classroom, pick up a copy of John Holt's "How Children Fail." It isn't based on observations made during the eighties, the seventies, or even the sixties. Much of what Holt observed took place in the late fifties, and yet it still seems every bit as valid today.

Through his personal experiences as a school teacher and his poignant yet startling vignettes of Nell and Herb and Emily, Holt painted the classroom as a world that was so odd and disorienting it seemed almost comical. It became clear to him that most children were not being encouraged to learn, but instead lived in fear of coming up with the wrong answer. Instead of creating, inventing and feeling bold, they paid meticulous attention to a teacher's body movements to see if they gave a clue to whether the word in question should go under the verb column or the noun column on the blackboard.

Holt saw the clear makings of an educational crisis in America's schools. The solution, he believed, did not lie in better standards or more tests, but in rethinking the whole dynamic between teacher and student. He had great faith in the ability of all children to learn, noting that there was "hardly an adult in a thousand, or ten thousand" who could learn as much about the world as a child did in the first three years of life. But what happened after that? Holt believed the problem lay with the often inflexible, almost illogical way in which they were taught.

"In many ways, we break down children's convictions that things make sense, or their hope that things may prove to make sense," he wrote. "We do it, first of all, by breaking up life into arbitrary and disconnected hunks of subject matter, which we then try to 'integrate' by such artificial and irrelevant devices as having children sing Swiss folk songs while they are studying the geography of Switzerland, or do arithmetic problems about rail-splitting while they are studying the boyhood of Lincoln."

To Holt, school did the very opposite of what it was intended to do: Instead of teaching kids to learn, it basically taught them not to learn. Instead of creating a thirst for knowledge, it only created discouragement and fear.

"We encourage kids to act stupidly," he wrote,

"not only by scaring and confusing them, but by boring them, by filling up their days with dull, repetitive tasks that make little or no claim on their attention or demands on their intelligence.

"Our hearts leap for joy at the sight of a roomful of children all slogging away at some imposed task, and we are all the more pleased and satisfied if someone tells us that the children don't really like what they are doing.

"By such means children are firmly established in the habit of using only a small part of their thinking capacity. They feel that school is a place where they must spend most of their time doing dull tasks in a dull way. Before long they are deeply settled in a rut of unintelligent behavior from which most of them could not escape even if they wanted to."

"How Children Fail" was published in 1964. It created a stir, selling over one million copies. Traditionalists were quick to condemn Holt as a radical who did not understand the roles and goals of education. But 27 years later, based on visits to dozens of schools around the country and interviews with hundreds of teachers, administrators and educational experts, it seems clear that American education has changed little since Holt observed it. If anything, it has gotten more complex because of the laundry list of social problems that many kids bring into the classroom.

Many of the outmoded aspects of teaching that

Holt observed are still being used. In too many schools, the dynamic between teacher and student is still dull and stunted. The classroom, instead of brimming with creativity, exudes dullness and boredom.

In his 1984 book "A Place Called School" John I. Goodlad, former Dean of the UCLA Graduate School of Education, concluded that teachers devoted much of their classroom time to one-sided lectures. Aided by a team of researchers who observed over 1,000 classrooms in 38 schools across the country, Goodlad found that five percent of class time was spent on direct questioning. Less than one percent, he concluded, was devoted to open questioning that called for higher-level mastery beyond memorization. Of the 150 minutes of instruction offered by a teacher during the course of a day, only seven minutes actually involved a teacher responding to a student's work.

The passivity of the classroom was almost frightening, prompting Goodlad to note how a colleague of his compared the typical American classroom to an Andy Warhol movie, "The Haircut."

For most of the film, the camera focuses on the face and head of a man getting a haircut. Absolutely nothing happens, and it is hard to stay awake. And then the man twitches, to the hysterical delight of the audience. In many ways the American classroom was much the same, where any "twitch," however trivial, became a welcome relief from the droning repetition.

"There was, in general, a lack of intensity—and particularly pleasure, enthusiasm, or sheer fun—in what students said about their classes," wrote Goodlad. "For many, it appeared, even being asked to respond to a question about the most important thing they had learned in a class came as a surprise.

"They often answered this question very much as they might answer a question about their country's major cities—as if the subject was something just beyond their domains of real interest and involvement."

Much of what went on in the classroom, Goodlad observed, was regurgitation. A teacher lectured, presented a body of material for the student to read, and then gave a test on it. Students, educational Darwinians down to the last drop, crammed for the test, got a good enough grade to survive and then promptly forgot most of what they had momentarily stored away.

Studies cited by Goodlad showed that students, within two years of taking an exam, had forgotten as much as 80 percent of the facts that were in it.

"Part of the brain, known as Magoun's brain, is stimulated by novelty. It appears to me that students spending 12 years in the schools we studied would be unlikely to experience much novelty. Does part of the brain just sleep, then?"

The answer to the school crisis, Goodlad believed, did not lie with more tests and more reliance on the memorization of facts. What should be stressed, Goodlad wrote, is the "importance of teachers finding ways to make subject matter relevant to students, to involve students in setting their own goals, to vary the ways of learning, to use approaches that employ all of the senses and to be sure that there are opportunities for relating the knowledge to experiences or actually using it."

Authors Arthur G. Powell, Eleanor Farrar and David K. Cohen in their book, "The Shopping Mall High School," wrote ". . . most of the foundation work of decent secondary education still remains to be done, seven or eight decades after the system began to take shape."

The most common purposes were getting through the period or covering the material, or some combination of the two.

"But why does one cover the material?" the authors asked. "If the only answer is that it has been mandated, or that it is in the book, then how can the material be taught well, or learned more than fleetingly?"

For students who are well-adjusted and highly disciplined, today's American school may have some benefit. Like squeezing juice from a lemon, they will find a way to learn. For many students, school only results in disengagement. The older a student gets, the more detached he seems to become from the learning process.

The early elementary school years are marked by warmth. The classrooms are bright and eclectic and cheerful. There is generally one teacher for all the subjects. Parents tend to be actively involved.

In part, elementary schools work because teachers are more child-oriented than their counterparts in middle school and high school. They tend to pay more attention to the whole child and realize that students thrive in a nurturing, creative environment. They also realize that "play" can become an effective way of getting a child to learn. By all accounts, the early years of elementary school work well. They provide students with the sense of community that they so desperately need in today's society. In many ways the education school resembles a small village— cozy, safe, connected.

Then something horrible happens. Parents become less active. Whereas they used to show up at school frequently during the elementary years, they are rarely present during the middle school years.

The classroom becomes bare and sterile, and the teachers themselves become disconnected from individual students. The classroom day changes radically as a child gets older. Instead of one teacher for all subjects, there is now a teacher for every subject. Tracking becomes more entrenched. So does labelling, and students become acutely aware of who is successful and who is not.

By the time high school comes around, the sense

of alienation is total. School is huge and impersonal and students have an increasingly hard time understanding the relevance of what is being taught. The demands are often negligible and as a result many students like school, not because they are learning anything, but because it is easy and pleasant and a great place to meet and greet friends. In an age of immediate gratification, they also show no responsibility for their own learning. They like being bored in the classroom. They have become used to it and they accept it as a natural part of school life.

Teachers, increasingly fearful of behavior problems in older students, make a subtle pact with them: Don't give me any trouble in the classroom and in return I'll demand nothing of you in the classroom.

These teachers tend to rely on textbooks and numbing lectures. Instead of actively engaging students in the process of learning, they give them worksheets to quietly look at until the bell rings.

It becomes a cycle of failure. Schools, instead of inspiring children and making them see why education is important and wonderful and exciting, do just the opposite.

For many children today, the turning point of their educational experience, whether they know it or not, is the age of nine. This is the year, most educators agree, in which the child subconsciously decides to opt in or opt out. Either he or she feels a sense of belonging to the school community and satisfaction with their personal progress within it, or they find it a place of frustration, failure and alienation and fall victim to the perceived pleasures of being someplace else. It is a pivotal decision, and it is made all the more wrenching by the process of disengagement that has already begun to take place.

"I found that fourth grade is the magic turning grade for rescue or, boy, you have to start playing catch-up, especially with young men," says Lorraine Monroe.

"That's the time they're comparing their sizes. That's the time when they're beginning to talk about prowess. If school can begin to play into those things, you can offset wanting to join a gang because your gang is here—you belong to the soccer gang. You're in the Little League gang, you're on the track team gang. And kids know what's a bad gang and what's a good gang—believe me, they know that.

"That's why you can't close school at 3 p.m. It's why you can't cut the supportive services of people who deal with the soul of kids because those are the things that save kids' lives. . . . Unless you're Einstein, a quadratic equation is not going to save your life."

But few schools in America today have that kind of irresistible power. Instead of becoming essential, the one thing in life a child cannot live without, they become just the opposite.

Just ask John Holt, who wrote the following in "How Children Fail":

"We destroy the disinterested (I do *not* mean uninterested) love of learning in children, which is so strong when they are small, by encouraging and compelling them to work for petty and contemptible rewards—gold stars, or papers marked 100 and tacked to the wall, or A's on report cards, or honor rolls, or dean's lists, or Phi Beta Kappa keys—in short, for the ignoble satisfaction of feeling that they are better than someone else.

"We encourage them to feel that the end aim of all they do in school is nothing more than to get a good mark on a test, or to impress someone with what they seem to know. We kill not only their curiosity, but their feeling that it is a good and admirable thing to be curious, so that by the age of ten most of them will not ask questions, and will show a good deal of scorn for the few who do."

These are depressing words, made all the more depressing by the fact that the factory structure of the classroom has changed little since Holt wrote about it more than 25 years ago.

And many of the narrowly focused reforms now being suggested, such as making students work harder, or holding teachers more accountable, may only exacerbate the school crisis instead of solving it.

Such reforms, wrote the authors of "The Shopping Mall High School," "skirt the question of what students have actually learned in favor of emphasizing superficial symbols of learning: what courses are taken, how many credits are accumulated, how much homework is given, how long a student spends in school. 'Standards' can thus be raised without much attention to actual performance.

"Despite periodic cries for quality or excellence, there is little agreement in the society or among high school educators that teaching students to use their minds fully is either needed by most youngsters or possible for them. . . . The schools have done a masterly job at selling the importance of high school attendance, but have failed in the attempt to sell to most students the value of working hard to learn to use one's mind."

FIVE

WHAT CAN HAPPEN

As EDUCATORS, POLITICIANS AND corporate leaders search for answers to the dilemma of America's schools, it has become fashionable to point eastward to the model of Japan.

The U.S. Department of Education has published a 95-page booklet on the subject, and the viewpoint is clear and obvious:

What has been successful in Japan can be successful here.

"Why should we Americans seek to distill lessons for ourselves from the experience of Japanese education? . . . Japanese education *works*," wrote William Bennett in 1987 when he was still the Secretary of Education. But it is debatable, perhaps even dangerous, to suggest that what works in Japan *should* work here. Research shows, for example, that Japanese schools are particularly difficult for "slow learners" and that women, who tend to play a second-class role in Japanese society, account for only 25 percent of university enrollment.

The pressure that is placed on Japanese teenagers

to get into the "right" college by passing the necessary college entrance examinations can also become intolerable. It is the "Harvard syndrome" at its worst, since a high-paying job in the corporate sector or with the government is virtually impossible unless a Japanese student has graduated from a top-ranking university.

But there is one aspect of Japanese schools that makes them enviable and also explains their enormous success.

It has nothing to do with what takes place inside the classroom. It isn't a matter of teaching the right courses, or the way the classroom is physically structured, or the types of demands placed on students. What is truly special about the Japanese school system, what is to be admired and coveted, is the place that the schoolhouse occupies in Japanese society.

In Japan, a child's entrance into first grade has become a deeply symbolic event, one that is filled with ritual and meaning and immediately embeds the school in the rockbed of the community. To mark the importance of the moment, children are sent gifts. They are supplied by parents with a desk and chair and a leather backpack that can cost as much as $150. On the first day of school, there is an elaborate ceremony filled with speeches by school and community officials. The impact of all of this is striking: When Japanese children enter that schoolhouse door for the very first time, they know they are embarking on the most important experience of their lives.

In the United States, it has become a cliché to say that education is important and should be central to the life of every child. Everyone believes it. But there is little to back up the feeling. When an American child enters the first grade, there is no welcoming speech from the school board or the mayor. There are no gifts and notes of congratulation. Beyond the lip service of saying that education is important, there is no sense of school being a key to anything. One of the most revealing and depressing trends of all about education has to do with what people expect from it.

The answer, more and more, appears to be nothing. American mothers believe more than Asian mothers that school success is the result of innate ability, according to a study by Harold Stevenson of the University of Michigan.

"The importance of hard work is diminished to the degree that parents believe that native ability is a basis for accomplishment," Stevenson wrote.

It means, in effect, that school is perceived as having no real value for those who don't have the "right stuff" academically. For those who are destined to do well, it works. For those who are not destined to do well, it doesn't work.

As a result, there is no sense of honor about school, no sense of excitement, no sense, as Lorraine Monroe so wonderfully puts it, that the "magic carpet ride" is about to begin.

Does it have to be that way? Can the pride that a

Japanese student feels in going to school be restored here? Can school be thought of as an institution with the power to ignite the imaginations and talents of everyone?

In various pockets around this country, there is evidence showing that American schools don't have to fail at all. There are educators who know they can make the schoolhouse as vital, as central to American life, as it is in Japan. They aren't doing it with a new salary structure for teachers. They aren't doing it with competency tests. They aren't doing it with a sudden influx of funds for sorely needed programs. They are doing it largely on the strength of their own determination and their own remarkable cult of personality.

Their efforts do not suggest that the ills of American education have been cured, because they are still isolated voices in the canyon. But their efforts do suggest that American education is not hopeless at all.

MIRACLE IN THE DESERT

The California terrain is dry and flat, still reminiscent of John Steinbeck's depiction of it in "The Grapes of Wrath." The school buildings themselves are low and sprawling, almost ranch-like, and at 8

A.M. kids trickle into school wearing the unofficial American uniform of T-shirt, pants and jackets.

Arvin High School, near Bakersfield, seems an unlikely place for innovation, an unlikely place for the kinds of wonderful things that *can* happen in American education. But such things are happening with a program called Project 2000.

Project 2000 isn't aimed at low achievers. It isn't aimed at high achievers. It is aimed at a very vulnerable segment in American education—the average student. In the "shopping mall" syndrome of American high schools, where a good education is possible, mostly for children with a strong developmental foundation, this is the group that often suffers the most. In many schools today, they get lost in the shuffle and their potential generally goes unfulfilled. They become the "forgotten half" and wrongly assume that college is for others kids, the kids who excel.

Project 2000 takes this so-called "middle group" and places them in a special program designed to make them ready for college. It is geared for ninth graders who range between the 25th and 65th percentile on various achievement tests. The emphasis of the program is on building self-esteem and confidence, improving skills through the guided use of technology and establishing a support network among parents, community and school. Parents are required to sign an agreement promising their cooperation and involvement in the project.

A major source of funding for the program is Ford Motor Company, and the relationship is perfect: Ford supplies the crucial funds to make Project 2000 possible, but it is educators who draw on their expertise and experience to create the optimum program.

Class size is kept to a maximum of 25, so students can get personal attention. Teachers, instead of individually teaching their own subjects, frequently meet to figure out ways to combine material and make it more relevant for students. School counselors have been given lighter work loads so they can devote two periods a day exclusively to Project 2000 students.

The program has been supplied with 25 computers and the computer lab is open not only during the week but also on Saturdays. It is not the computers per se, but how they're used that makes this special. Parents come to the school to take computer classes on weekends, often in connection with their children. Sometimes, in fact, it is the children who are doing the teaching.

The special attention that these students are receiving has had an enormous impact. They obviously like the program. Once thought to be on a track to nowhere, many of them are blossoming. Now that school has a purpose in their lives, now that they see the potential of it, they like being pushed. Demands upon them make sense because school makes sense. Their favorite teacher was someone young who could identify with many of their needs. That wasn't surprising. But the students also gravitated towards her because she yelled at them when they weren't pushing themselves to the limit.

"It makes me feel proud to be in it," one student of Project 2000 told us.

"It's great, it's exciting," said another.

"It's a miracle," said another.

COULDN'T BE DONE

When John Dow Jr. tried it during his first year as the Superintendent of Schools for the City of New Haven, they went crazy.

Some tried to get him fired. Some were livid. Some simply refused to go along with it. How dare he try to do this?

Dow knew what he was doing was controversial. But he also knew that in times of crisis, the remedies must sometimes be drastic as well.

He knew that one of the crucial ways of achieving success in school was through parent involvement. Knowing that was one thing. Actually getting a parent to come to school and take an interest in their child's education was another. So he did what he had to do: He required parents to come to school for an orientation session as a *condition* of enrolling their children in the New Haven schools. As Dow told us:

"[It] almost got me fired the first year I was here. But we wanted to make a statement to parents that irrespective of how old your youngster is, you need to be involved.

"The first few years of schooling set a tone that does not change. And I have to speak for New Haven because we have tracked that. And so, what we are saying is that we have to educate, we have to manipulate, and ultimately, we have to do whatever's necessary to encourage participation.

"And those individuals who said that requiring parents to come to enroll their children was wrong, we have proved *them* wrong. Because there is not a parent I know of who does not want to see his or her children succeed. Now, they may not know how to make that happen, but they do want that.

"I think all institutions that have a vested interest in child advocacy must do whatever is necessary. Not in a punitive way, but clearly understand we're only fooling ourselves, and really shortchanging our children, if we don't make a stand and insist that we do things that we know will ultimately help children in the long term."

The requirement of parent involvement is just one of the many changes that Dow has made in successfully turning around the schools. There are school-based clinics for health and nutrition problems. The SAT test, crucial to college admission, has become a requirement for all students. Dr. Dow believes that this sends an important signal to every child that college *is* a possibility for him or her.

Dow also encourages high school teachers to take their classes on trips to colleges far and wide. "Wealthy parents," he says, "take their children away for weekends to tour lovely campuses and to encourage them to think about the kind of environment that might be right for them. It expands the kids' sense of possibilities and encourages them to feel that going to college is the natural course their lives should follow. Why shouldn't we create the same sense of possibilities for kids from middle- and lower-income environments?"

To further encourage students to go to college, the district pays the costs of the first application. In 1985, about 45 percent of New Haven's students were accepted by colleges and post-secondary institutions. In 1988 the figure had gone up to 73 percent.

"I think it's very important that everyone understands that urban schools can change if we take all of the positive and good things that we know about schools, irrespective of where they are and try to implement those criteria in urban America," says Dow.

PREVENTION, NOT CRISIS

The little boy had taken a sudden downturn for the worse. His performance in school dropped sharply.

He seemed agitated and distressed, gravely troubled by something. But he wouldn't say what it was.

In many schools, the problem would have gone unheeded until it was too late. He would have been chalked off as another hopeless case, another child pulled down by the streets, or drugs, or a horrible home.

But this little boy was lucky. He was in an elementary school that was run under the auspices of Jim Comer and the Yale Intervention Program.

The mental health team at the school, comprised of the school nurse, the principal, a child psychologist, a social worker and someone with expertise in learning disorders, discussed the little boy during their weekly meeting. They obviously recognized that there was a problem and they knew they had to do something about it before it became a crisis.

The mental health team discovered that the little boy was living by himself in the projects. The social worker went to where he lived and made arrangements for a neighbor to take care of him.

The child psychologist talked to him and found out the little boy was convinced that his mother had gone to the hospital and had died. The school principal made some phone calls and found out that it was true—the little boy's mother had gone to the hospital.

But she wasn't sick. . . . She wasn't dying. . . . She was having a baby.

The mental health team made arrangements for the

little boy to talk to his mother. Reassured that she was perfectly fine, and safely situated in a protective household, he started to function in school again.

"A staff that understands child development and how to organize and manage their school building as a social system is best able to create a climate that facilitates learning among the greatest number of students," Comer wrote.

"Unfortunately, it is precisely in these critical areas—child development and school management—that the instruction of teachers and administrators is most deficient."

As a result, when a student acts up in school, or suddenly pays no attention to his school work, it is usually attributed to his socioeconomic background. He is written off as someone who can't learn. School, instead of becoming a lifesaver, becomes just another source of embitterment and rage.

"When bankers lose money, they make an adjustment," Comer wrote. "When products are defective, manufacturing firms examine both the material and the process. When a patient remains ill or dies, the physician or the medical profession searches for new cures. But when students underachieve and act out in response to their frustration—particularly if the student has been designated as less capable or desirable by society—school staffs often assume that the problem lies in the student or his or her family, income, race or religion, not in the process of education in the building."

During his involvement at several elementary schools in New Haven, Comer has refused to make the same mistake. All kids can learn, but not all kids start at the same level in terms of developmental skills, whether it be listening quietly to a story, processing information, or coping with disappointment. Children who are prone to rages or angry outbursts in the classroom or are constant behavioral problems are not incorrigible. They are not young criminal types just waiting to be old enough to handle a gun. Often, the way they act at school is a response to what is happening outside of school. They may be suffering from divorce. They may be suffering from abuse. They may be suffering from the lack of any consistent anchor in their lives.

". . . if we could think of the child as needing a certain kind of experience to prepare him or her for school, and if that child is receiving it, fine, we can reinforce it at school," says Comer. "If a child is not receiving it, then the child *must* receive it at school.

"The child must be helped to handle his or her aggressive energy, and channel it, learn how to control himself or herself. Learn how to interact socially with other people. [There is a] whole series of things that can be taught in school, if we recognize these are the needs."

In addition to a mental health team, Comer has also instituted a school-based management team particularly sensitive to child development and relationship issues. The team is made up of administrators, teachers and parents. Because of the structure of it, decision-making doesn't come from a single authority figure but from a variety of participants, each with a different perspective on what children need to develop.

Comer has also put a parents' program into place. This program is essential as well, for it breeds trust in the educational process. Parents no longer feel alienated by school. They no longer perceive it as an institution outside the reach of their own world. Instead they feel a part of it. The parents' program is not some lip-service gesture, but a group that has direct input into the school's policies and plans.

To help kids with particular emotional problems, something called a "discovery room" was started at one of the schools. Everything about the room—the teaching, the equipment—was designed to give children more positive feelings about themselves and to override the negative feelings that were causing them to reject school. Among other concepts, kids were taught how to "fail" and not become unraveled by it, but rather to accept failure as something that happens to everyone on the way to success. Children were also encouraged, but not pushed, to talk openly about anything, whether it be anxiety in school, difficulties at home, death, race or illness.

The "Two-Years-With-the-Same Teacher" program was also instituted, on the common-sense theory that one of the most anxiety-inducing parts of school for any child, particularly young ones, is change. In Comer's case, the idea of the program came to him when a teacher mentioned that a student in her class, frightened, underachieving and withdrawn, had actually smiled at her. It was a wonderful breakthrough, but with only a month left in the school year, it seemed almost bittersweet. "Oh, if I could only have her longer," the teacher lamented. The comment prompted Comer to realize that the traditional method of a new teacher every year didn't make sense, particularly in an increasingly unstable society. So he switched to the two-year concept.

By establishing programs such as these, the results have been astounding. King Elementary, one of the worst schools in New Haven on the basis of achievement scores, is now one of the best. Another Comer school, Brennan Elementary, recently scored the highest of 722 schools in the United States on a mathematics examination. The results were so astounding that the sponsors of the test automatically assumed that Brennan was a private school.

In a study of several schools in Benton Harbor, Michigan, that are using the Comer approach, suspensions dropped eight percent. In comparison, suspensions district-wide went *up* 34 percent.

Because of results such as these, Comer's theories are now gaining widespread support. In 1990, the Rockefeller Foundation announced that it was making a five-year commitment to help spread the word of Comer around the country.

"Dr. Comer's work builds bridges," Hugh B. Price, a Rockefeller Foundation vice president, told *The New York Times*. "One is built from the parent to the school, and one out from the school to the children." But it is Comer himself who articulates best what a school in today's America must be:

"There is an assumption that learning is a kind of mechanical process—that you give information, kids take it in, they process it and give it back to you—or store it and remember it forever—and can act on it. That's not true. It is much more complicated. The reason we learn has a lot to do with our past experiences and our relationships with important others. We are motivated to learn out of relationships.

". . . Many of the people, maybe most of the people commenting on what education should or shouldn't be and so on, are from middle- and upper-income families or well-functioning families. And they assume that all the children had experiences just like they had in school and are just as ready for school as they were when they went to school. You take that assumption, plus the assumption that it's a mechanical process, and then all you have to do is focus on teaching, and the children will learn.

"Well, it's not a mechanical process, relationships are important, and most children, many children, the ones we're concerned about the most, have not had the pre-school experiences that allow them to achieve."

FORCED TO THINK

On a sunny June day, ninth graders participating in The Coalition of Essential Schools program in Bronxville High School settle into the desks arranged in the horseshoe setting that is customary for this class, squarely facing each other, with their three teachers seated at the base of the "U."

The seating arrangement itself seems reflective of what must have gone on all year in this classroom. "Exposed" in this face-to-face way, it would be literally impossible to nod off undetected, or otherwise drift away from what was going on in class.

At this point in the semester, it seems clear that these teenagers don't want to disconnect from what's happening. Each one seems fully, vibrantly, actively *there*.

These students have elected to participate in a special interdisciplinary course at Bronxville High School, situated in a tiny, affluent enclave outside of New York City. Given the polite, well-dressed, well-bred look of these kids, one might expect them to be strong "performers." But simple performance is not what this Coalition program is all about, as is about to be evidenced.

Today is the day that the students are to demonstrate their mastery of the subjects they have explored all year, under the guidance of an interdisciplinary teaching team. For two double back-to-back periods scheduled several times a week throughout the semester, these teenagers have met with their art, social studies and English teachers to wrestle with the ideas and events which shaped their culture, in a course called the History of Western Civilization.

The students will not be taking any final exam. Instead, they have been required to develop a thesis based on a theme each has worked out with his or her teaching team, and then to express the core idea of that thesis through a piece of art or literature of the student's own design.

This is the first day in a series in which each student will reveal his or her core idea "project," and discuss its meaning before the class, the teachers and the principal. Students' evaluations will be determined by the extent to which the teaching team believes they have demonstrated a mastery of the coursework through the written thesis itself, their discussion of it and the piece of art or literature they have created to express it.

Today, each student speaks for about 20 minutes. Some are more articulate than others, but hardly anyone falters or fumbles or digresses to disguise a lack of knowledge. In almost every case, the kids speak with the confidence and enthusiasm that stems from having understood and internalized their subject matter.

The ideas they have developed are powerful ones. One young man presents an illustrated piece he has written entitled "The Power Game," developing his concept that throughout the course of Western Civilization, power and authority have been sequentially transferred from deities, to monarchs, to the people. He relates this concept to the then-current tragedy in Tiananmen Square.

A young woman reveals a dramatic piece of sculpture she has created to express her thesis on "Ostracism" as a shaping force in Western history. Others read poems, discuss paintings, read their short stories aloud.

The presentations are provocative and impressive. At the end of the class, the atmosphere is celebratory. The presenters don't need to hear the teachers' reactions to know that they have done a good job. *They* know they know what they're doing.

Afterwards, Bronxville High School's principal, Alan Guma, explains that the Coalition Program is an "experiment" in his school, and a fragile one at that. "In many ways," he says, "it's easier to pull this off in East Harlem," referring to a Coalition School in an impoverished section of New York City. "Things are so bad in the inner cities that there's a greater receptivity to innovation. People feel things can only get better. But in communities such as this one, expectations *start out* so high people are afraid to rock the boat.

"The parents and kids who choose to participate in this program have a lot of conviction about learning.

Others are waiting to see evidence that kids who learn this way get high SAT scores and are accepted by good colleges."

In their book "The Shopping Mall High School," the authors Powell, Farrar and Cohen challenge schools, parents and students to take risks in return for a greater commitment to learning.

"A good school must be morally averse to low expectations," they write. "Inside classrooms, the absence of students' skill in using their minds should never be an excuse for not trying to develop that skill."

They go on to say:

"It is especially crucial to substitute personal attention for anonymous individualization. Even if some teenagers say they prefer anonymity because they feel rejected, dejected or just shy, abandoning them to make their own way should not be tolerated. Even if high schools continue a studied neutrality about what knowledge is of most worth, or what ethical principles are essential beyond basic civility, they need not be neutral about anonymous individualization. Parents who disagree about other things, or are passive and uninformed about school, usually agree that they want their children known seriously as individuals by key adults in school."

Ted Sizer's personal mission is to force all the stakeholders in education to think hard about the *role* of that education and to arrive at the conclusion that teaching students how to use their minds well should be our priority, first and foremost.

But a true commitment to that goal requires a major reorientation in much of the current thinking about educational reform.

Sizer calls for a new focus:

"American schools have been battered over the last decade by steady criticism that has left teachers and administrators confused, embarrassed and angry. They are blamed for failing to overcome the results of poverty, the drug crisis, the economic dislocation of communities and changing morals. They are blamed for failing to be creative enough to meet the challenges of new technology and the communication revolution. There are many conflicting messages in this criticism. Teachers are told to be creative, but are warned to stick to a predetermined curriculum and to get back to 'basics.' They are told to train adolescents to meet the challenges of a complex, changing society by teaching them in a rigid and authoritarian style.

"This initiative offers another message: Teach to the human capacity to learn, to create, to synthesize ideas, to theorize, to make order out of chaos, to invent and be active—in effect to use one's mind richly and well. We must teach thoughtfully, allowing the students to do the hard work, to discover the formulas, to test their knowledge through Socratic challenge and to research and defend their ideas and findings. We must provoke in all students a habit of thoughtfulness, and through these students, create a society of thinkers, doers and dreamers—a society fit for a 21st century democracy."

PUTTING IT ALL TOGETHER

Some schools work simply because they are inhabited by an extraordinary group of educators who care a great deal about today's kids, and are determined to do whatever it takes to help them develop and learn.

Other schools work because they are informed, guided and supported by a larger concept, model or network, such as Comer's and Sizer's.

But, however they came into being, schools that work are increasingly being driven by the same imperative:

> *Expect a great deal* of children and then give them *whatever support* they need to meet those expectations.

Lorraine Monroe has a strategy for accomplishing this goal, something she calls the Monroe Doctrine: *"You can't leave anything to chance."*

The people in schools that work don't sit back and *hope* that a child connects with a caring adult; they make sure that it happens. They don't wait for problems to get out of control; they deal with early signs of trouble as soon as they spot them.

Schools that work recognize that the assumptions that held true for children in the thirties, forties and fifties cannot be depended on anymore. These schools do not assume that a child has learned about quiet time at home before he or she gets to school. They do not assume that children know how to behave in a classroom setting. Most important, they don't write off a child because he or she doesn't know these things. They recognize that school has to be the place to teach and nurture them.

The *one place* that insures productive human development.

SIX

WHAT MUST HAPPEN

THERE IS A CRISIS in the schools.

We are failing our children.

They are stunning, shocking words. But they are true.

Throughout the course of our history, schools have traditionally shaped our beliefs, our hopes, our dreams, our very faith in democracy and equality.

> "If a nation expects to be ignorant and free, in a state of civilization, it expects what never was and never will be. . . . I look to the diffusion of light and education as the resource most to be relied on for ameliorating the degraded condition, promoting the virtue, and advancing the happiness of man. . . .
>
> "When I contemplate the immense advances in science and discoveries in the arts which have been made within the period of my life, I look forward with confidence to equal advances by the present generation, and have no doubt they will consequently be as much wiser than we have been, as we than our fathers were, and they than the burners of witches."

The author of those words, Thomas Jefferson, knew the power of education to keep our nation alive, vital and thriving. It formed the most solid rock of society, the dividing line between virtue and indifference, compassion and hatred, decency and contempt. It is a cornerstone we cannot afford to lose, and yet we are in danger of doing just that.

What difference does it make?

Forget the brain drain that has become the universal lament of corporate America. Forget the acute shortage of skilled workers. Just take a look at our nation's overcrowded jails. What you will find is a group of individuals who have a disturbing characteristic in common—a failed education.

In a study by the New York Department of Correctional Services of 10,250 inmates, 80 percent entered the system without a high school diploma, 50 percent functioned below the eighth grade level in reading and 73 percent below the eighth grade level in math. Had more attention been paid to these individuals when they were younger, had school been a positive experience instead of a negative one, would it have had any impact? The answer is obvious.

"Clearly, the public should realize that the crime problem begins at a child's early age," wrote Ernest M. May, the former board chairman of Montclair State College, in a letter to *The New York Times*. ". . . all available means should be enlisted to see to it that the child's pathway leads to constructive drug-free citizenship, rather than to crime."

There are pockets of hope around the country

when it comes to education. But they are aberrations, programs that don't naturally flow from the system but seem to blossom almost in spite of it. These programs are getting more and more attention in the media, but they still serve an infinitesimal portion of America's 40 million students.

In most places around the country, the schoolhouse is not a beacon, but a drab, sterile institution that has little relevance to those who participate in it. In Japan, going to school is treated as a sacred event. Nothing is more important and it is hard to think of any institution in Japanese society that has more prestige and power. In the United States, the American educational system seems about ready to implode.

Teachers are worried and frustrated. They are understandably tired of being blamed for everything that has gone wrong. They see kids with problems that are unimaginable, almost terrifying, and they don't know what to do. Students are bored and rudderless. In a world where every social institution has split apart, their lives today have no anchors, no fixtures. They go to school and it joins their list of places that have no purpose. They sense that their teachers don't like them, may even have contempt for them. They tend to see school as a social event, not an event that will prepare them for life. Parents are concerned, but simply don't know what to do.

In a society in which institutional and personal

connections have deteriorated, school reflects just another progressive unraveling of meaningful connections.

The crisis is real, but it is not permanent. The crisis is shocking, but it is not irreversible. There are enough examples out there, whether it's the desert of California, the inner city of New Haven, or the lake shores of Wisconsin, to prove that American education can work again.

To make these isolated success stories universal, the American school must be overhauled. It can no longer be a place that just teaches academics. The ABCs are just a piece of the increasingly intricate puzzle.

School has to become the one institution in our society which *guarantees* that every child can experience a sense of belonging, a sense of worth, a sense of purpose. It has to be the place that *guarantees* that every child is provided with the physical, emotional and psychological support that is essential to human development.

Our public school system still represents our best hope for realizing that goal.

In many cases, it represents our only hope.

Consider what *could happen* even in our most troubled communities to make schools work—to rescue children and their families:

Schools *could be* a resource to parents from birth or even conception.

- Mothers would go there for prenatal counseling.
- Mothers and fathers would go there to get General Equivalency Diplomas (GEDs).
- There would be an in-house psychologist, as well as an in-house social worker, to help counsel families about parenting and about learning and development for all family members. Before a child was ever born, the family would already be going in and out of school all the time and they would see it as the one indispensable place in their lives, the one place to go to for support, for counseling, for job training, for everything that is important to life.
- The barriers leading to suspicion and alienation would be broken down. The "cultural gap" between home and school that tears so many kids apart would be eliminated.

Schools and school people *could be* accessible to families and children whenever they were needed.

- Schools would be open all day, all year.
- Single working parents could rest assured that their children were off the street until they get home from work. Children from dysfunctional families would have a shelter, a place where stable healthy adults could care for them, and

see to it they were placed in protective environments. Children and teachers would not
lose precious ground during the long summer
break or on weekends. Relationships formed
between children and school people would be
what they *should be,* what they must be: *lifesav-
ing connections children can unconditionally count
on.*

- School would be the lifeline. The safety net.
The fail-safe place.

Children *could be* given every chance to succeed, from
the beginning.

- Schooling would begin for children as early as
age 2 or 2½. Children would be given the
developmental skills they need in order to
enter first grade fully capable of learning. Fed-
erally sponsored programs such as Head Start
have clearly demonstrated that early intervention gives children the foundation they need
to succeed throughout their school years. Children suffering from developmental disorders
could be helped before the problems become
debilitating.
- Children would be encouraged to think of
themselves as successful *learners* from the
start.

Throughout school, learning *could be* humanized, de-mechanized.

- Classes would be smaller. Teachers would come in contact with fewer students, so that they would get to know each one better. Teachers would stay with one group of kids for two, maybe three years.
- There would be flexible scheduling so that kids and teachers could make the most out of their classroom time instead of being at the mercy of the school bell. One period might be 90 minutes, another 120 minutes. In some cases, the teaching of subjects would be compartmentalized; in others, a variety of different subjects would be taught at once to make the material more relevant and alive.
- Teachers would have had better training in child development. They would get more help in breaking through to kids who haven't learned how to learn.

Personal support *could be* an integral part of the learning process.

- Time would be set aside to insure that students have every opportunity to form relationships with caring adults—lay volunteers, teachers, psychologists, mentors, coaches. Kids could talk about themselves, their home lives, their school work.

- Counseling would not be a peripheral part of the educational process, as it is now, nor would it be a measure reserved for extreme cases or situations. Relating to individual students, and helping them work their way through problems and challenges would be what it *must* be: an integral part of what every child's school experience is all about.

Some of these strategies may be more or less appropriate in individual schools, while in *some* schools, every one of these elements and more may be essential.

The answer does not lie in any prescribed structure or schedule, but in the adoption of a different *concept* of what schools must be and what schools must do.

There is only one valid guide to what a particular school in a particular community must be like.

It is not precedent, or what has been done historically.

It is not some model forcibly imposed from some distant and different culture, be it the corporation, the marketplace or Japan. It is not even the opinions of legislators or schools boards.

The only valid guide to what a particular school in a particular community should be and do is this:

Given the realities of their lives, what do these children need to develop, learn and become the masters of their own destinies?

Whatever the specific course of action we each choose to take, we must begin now, because even those who have the highest hopes for education are worried.

All her life Lorraine Monroe has been an optimist when it comes to schooling. All her life she has been one of those educators who knows that things can happen if you want them to, that kids can routinely produce miracles with the proper alchemy of love and respect and demand.

But for the first time in her life, Lorraine Monroe doesn't feel that ebullience. A whole new generation of children is beginning to enter the schools now. They are the sons and daughters of crack users, and she doesn't know if an already burdened system can handle it.

It isn't enough to dream anymore and make wonderful plans on paper. It is a matter of doing whatever it takes to make dreams about education come true, not for her sake, but for the sake of every American child. Our country depends on it. Our very future depends on it.

"I'm scared," says Lorraine Monroe. "I'm an optimist, and I'm scared."

SEVEN

WHAT YOU CAN DO

SOCIAL REVOLUTIONS SUCCEED WHEN a good idea becomes recognized, accepted and embraced by the population at large. This process can take centuries or years or it can happen in weeks. The speed of change depends on the commitment of the "change-makers" and how quickly the broader group is exposed to the new ideas and becomes willing to adopt them.

We cannot wait decades or years for the ideas that can rescue our kids to spread. We need a powerful surge of new energy to change our children's and our nation's dismal future. Since you have read this far, you are obviously concerned about the fate of children. The chances are good that you would like to be involved in improving their chances of having successful and productive lives.

The health of your community is based to a great extent on the quality of its youth's education. You can imagine how much better any community would be if a caring, involved, successful school were operating there.

As you know by now, the solutions are out there. They exist. The model schools are out there. They exist. The model teachers and principals are out there.

You can help immediately by spreading the word of their successes, supporting the innovators, so more people can pick up their beat and march to their different drum.

The benefits to your community, to American business and the nation are many. But those benefits are secondary. The greater purpose is the fundamental social principle of treating our children as total human beings, not just as young people who need to pass tests.

Today, more than ever, young people need education in the broadest, truest sense. They need to understand how to cope with and to progress in life. To do that they need stability in their lives and the sure knowledge that people understand and care about them as human beings and are doing something about their needs.

This change will not happen by itself. It needs a catalyst. You can be a catalyst.

1. First and foremost you can let people know the real problem and the real solution. Start by sharing this book with people of influence. Make it clear that our kids are being affected by an enormous tide of social

change and not just by the incidental failure of our schools. Explain that our schools do not have the structure, skills or resources to deal with this change.

Use the media. Write letters to the editor of your local paper, to television and radio stations—whatever you feel capable of doing. Push to see that responsible reporting about the educational problem and its solution is done. Distribute copies of this book to members of your school board and the local superintendent.

2. To be effective, find out where the good ideas are being put into practice. Visit the schools or create teams made up of teachers, administrators, parents and business people to visit, study or even work in schools where the new and productive methods are being used.

If you are a business person, you could delegate one or two members of your organization to report firsthand on how the schools operate in your area and what contributions your company might make.

Often significant changes are not expensive. Consider setting up a "principal's fund"—a discretionary fund that a principal can use to enable children to have expansive and important experiences for which even a little money is often impossible to get. You can underwrite the costs of a visiting team for one or more of the selected schools.

It is critical that outsiders become involved. The system cannot heal itself. You, as an outsider, can perform a revolutionary role as a catalyst.

3. Support the model schools in any way you can. Once you find the model school operating in your community, or one that is trying to become one, you can support it in many ways. If you run a business you might become a "partner" with the school. See how you can bring your business, administrative or managerial skills to help achieve the school's goals. Frankly, business people have the experience, the directness and the energy that can mesh with the skills of school administrators.

Communicate with parents. They have a stronger vested interest than anyone else and, therefore, a greater need to be involved, and a great ability to attract other parents into what can become a formidable force of volunteers.

Schools need moral, political and financial support and media attention as well. Would your company underwrite some form of communication which illustrates the problem and some of the solutions? They can range all the way from an internal newsletter to a brochure to a paid ad to a media program.

There are teachers' colleges listed in the Appendix which have committed themselves to preparing teachers to educate children in the ways described in this book. You can support these colleges.

In summary, it is a unique and dangerous time for American education and for our schools. It calls for unique solutions.

You now know that the techniques to solve the problem are available. The programs we have discussed will alter the very fabric of our society and are designed to provide the emotional support a child desperately needs as he or she grows.

You can be a catalyst. You can gather like-minded people who want to implement what is being done in the model schools. You can get business leaders involved in making change and urge them to become contributors to the effort.

Finally, most important, you can get people stirred up and enthused about the prospect of real and positive change. We will all benefit from your help. So, celebrate the successes, be part of the solution. Spread the word. Help. Please.

APPENDIX

NATIONAL REFORMERS:

Dr. James P. Comer
Yale Child Study Center
Director, The School
   Development Program
230 South Frontage Road
New Haven, CT 06520
(203) 785-6227

Dr. James Boger
Yale Child Study Center
Coordinator of
   Intervention and
   Training
230 South Frontage Road
New Haven, CT 06520
(203) 785-6227

Dr. Theodore R. Sizer
Chairman, Coalition of
   Essential Schools
Brown University
One Davol Square
Providence, RI 02903
(401) 863-3384

Edward Ziegler, Ph.D.
Sterling Professor of
   Psychology
Box 11A Yale Station
Yale University
New Haven, CT 06520
(203) 432-4576

Dr. Lorraine Monroe
Founder and Former
   Director
Center for Minority
   Achievement
Bank Street College of
   Education
610 West 112th Street
New York, NY 10025
(212) 222-6700
(212) 662-0662

INNOVATIVE SCHOOLS

The Commissioner of Education or other chief education officer in your state should be able to identify innovative local schools. (A listing of Chief State School Officers is included in this Appendix.)

Depending upon where you live or travel, you may also have the opportunity to familiarize yourself with one or many of the 165 schools currently committed to adopting James Comer's School Development Program. Here's a listing of those schools by location:

SDP School Profile: Number of Schools by School Level					
School District	Year Began	Number of Elem. Schools	Number of Jr. High Schools	Number of High Schools	Total
Benton Harbor, MI	1983	15	2	1	18
Chicago, IL	1990	4			4
Hartford, CT	1990	6			6
Lee County, AK	1987	4	1	1	6
Leavenworth, KS	1987	8			8
New Haven, CT	1968	26	8	6	40
Norfolk, VA	1983	12	4		16
P.G. County, MD	1985	30	12		42
Seattle, WA	1990	3			3
San Diego, CA	1990	3			3
Springfield, MA	1990	4			4
Sarasota, FL	1988	4			4
Topeka, KS	1988	5			5
Washington, DC	1990	6			6
Total		130	27	8	165

Dr. Comer's office will be happy to give you the precise locations of those schools that most interest you.

COALITION OF ESSENTIAL SCHOOLS MEMBER SCHOOLS

Ted Sizer's group has also agreed to help locate local schools that are part of The Coalition of Essential Schools. Here's a general listing:

ARKANSAS
SPRINGDALE HIGH SCHOOL
Springdale, AR 72764
  Harry Wilson, Principal
  (501) 750-8832

CALIFORNIA
MID-PENINSULA HIGH
  SCHOOL
870 North California
  Avenue
Palo Alto, CA 94303
  Philip Bliss, Chairman
  (415) 493-5910

CONNECTICUT
AVON HIGH SCHOOL
510 West Avon Road
Avon, CT 06001
  Dr. Michael Buckley,
    Principal
  (203) 673-2551

Avon District Office:
  Dr. Herbert F. Pandiscio
  Superintendent
  Dr. Crisanne Colgan
  Sr. Director of
    Instruction
  (203) 678-0482

FLORIDA
NOVA BLANCHE FOREMAN
  SCHOOL
3521 Davie Road
Davie, FL 33314
  Larry Katz, Principal
  (305) 370-1788

NOVA EISENHOWER SCHOOL
6501 SW 39 Street
Davie, FL 33314
  Mary Mitchell, Principal
  (305) 370-1777

NOVA MIDDLE SCHOOL
3602 SW College Avenue
Fort Lauderdale, FL 33314
  Suzanne Alvord,
    Principal
  (305) 370-1758

NOVA HIGH SCHOOL
3600 SW College Avenue
Fort Lauderdale, FL 33314
  Larry Insel, Principal
  (305) 370-1700
  Nova Schools Coordinator
  Pat Ciabotti
  Nova High School
  (305) 370-8341

UNIVERSITY SCHOOL OF
  NOVA UNIVERSITY
7500 SW 36th Street
Fort Lauderdale, FL 33314
  James Byer, Headmaster
  (305) 476-1900
  Jerry Chermak,
    Coordinator
  (305) 476-1904

IOWA
METRO HIGH SCHOOL
1212 7th Street, SE
Cedar Rapids, IA 52401

Mary Wilcynski,
  Principal
(319) 398-2193

KENTUCKY
*Jefferson County Public
  Schools*
BALLARD HIGH SCHOOL
6000 Brownsboro Road
Louisville, KY 40222
  Sandy Allen, Principal
  Norman McKenna,
    Coordinator
  (502) 473-8206

DOSS HIGH SCHOOL
7601 St. Andrews Church
  Road
Louisville, KY 40214
  Gordon Milby, Principal
  Carole Sanders,
    Coordinator
  (502) 473-8239

FAIRDALE HIGH SCHOOL
1001 Fairdale Road
Louisville, KY 40118
  Marilyn Hohmann,
    Principal

Brenda Butler,
Coordinator
(502) 473-8248

PLEASURE RIDGE PARK
HIGH SCHOOL
5901 Greenwood Road
Pleasure Ridge Park, KY
40258
Charles Miller, Principal
Susie Garrett,
Coordinator
(502) 473-8311

SENECA HIGH SCHOOL
3510 Goldsmith Lane
Louisville, KY 40220
John Whiting, Principal
Judy Phillips,
Coordinator
(502) 473-8323

MAYME S. WAGGENER HIGH
SCHOOL
330 South Hubbards Lane
St. Matthews, KY 40207
Donna Ludwig,
Principal
Harry Orten,
Coordinator
(502) 473-8340

Jefferson County Schools
Coordinator
Debbie Riggs
Jefferson County Public
Schools
Gheens Professional
Development
Academy
4425 Preston Highway
Louisville, KY 40213
(502) 473-3494

MAINE
PORTLAND HIGH SCHOOL
284 Cumberland Avenue
Portland, ME 04101
Barbara Anderson,
Principal
(207) 874-8250

MARYLAND
BRYN MAWR SCHOOL
109 West Melrose
Baltimore, MD 21210
Barbara Chase,
Headmistress
Marlene David,
Coordinator
(301) 323-8800

PARK HEIGHTS STREET
ACADEMY
3901 Park Heights Avenue
Baltimore, MD 21215
   Deneauvo Robinson,
      Headmaster
   Betty J. Foy,
      Coordinator
   (301) 367-3446

WALBROOK HIGH SCHOOL
200 Fonthill Anveue
Baltimore, MD 21223
   Samuel Billups,
      Principal
   Marian Finney,
      Coordinator
   (301) 396-0723

MASSACHUSETTS
ANDOVER HIGH SCHOOL
Andover, MA 01810
   Wilbur Hixson,
      Principal
   Craig Simpson,
      Coordinator
   (508) 470-1707

BRIMMER AND MAY SCHOOL
69 Middlesex Road
Chestnut Hill, MA 02167

Anne Reenstierna,
   Headmistress
Nancy Echlov, Co-
   Coordinator
Judy Guild, Co-
   Coordinator
(617) 566-7462

MASSACHUSETTS
ADVANCED STUDIES
PROGRAM (SUMMER
ONLY)
MILTON ACADEMY
170 Centre Street
Milton, MA 02186
   Chuck Burdick, Director
   (617) 698-7800

MISSOURI
PARKWAY SOUTH HIGH
   SCHOOL
801 Hanna Road
Manchester, MO 63021
   Craig Larson, Principal
   Patrick Conley,
      Coordinator
   (314) 394-8300

THE WHITFIELD SCHOOL
175 South Mason Road
St. Louis, MO 63141

Mary Burke,
Headmistress
Adrienne Lyss,
Coordinator
(314) 434-5141

NEW HAMPSHIRE
THAYER HIGH SCHOOL
43 Parker Street
Winchester, NH 03470
Dennis Littky, Principal
(603) 239-4381

NEW YORK
ADELPHI ACADEMY
8515 Ridge Boulevard
Brooklyn, NY 11209
Clinton Vickers,
Headmaster
Greg Borman,
Coordinator
(718) 238-3308

ALTERNATIVE COMMUNITY
SCHOOL
111 Chestnut Street
Ithaca, NY 14850
Dave Lehman, Principal
(607) 274-2183

BRONXVILLE HIGH SCHOOL
Pondfield Road
Bronxville, NY 10708
Alan Guma, Principal
Judy Oksner, Co-
Coordinator
Joanne Duffy, Co-
Coordinator
(914) 337-5600

CENTRAL PARK EAST
SECONDARY SCHOOL
1573 Madison Avenue
New York, NY 10029
Deborah Meier,
Director
Herb Rosenfeld,
Coordinator
(212) 860-8935

FOX LANE HIGH SCHOOL
Rte. 172, South Bedford
Road
Bedford, NY 10506
Robert A. Mackin,
Principal
(914) 241-6065
Glynn Meggison,
Coordinator
(914) 241-6070

IRONDEQUOIT HIGH
SCHOOL
260 Cooper Road
Rochester, NY 14617
Stewart Agor, Principal
Dana Meredith,
Coordinator
(716) 266-7351

JOHN JAY HIGH SCHOOL
Katonah, NY 10536
John Chambers,
Principal
Christine Krause,
Coordinator
(914) 763-3126

SCARSDALE ALTERNATIVE
SCHOOL
45 Wayside Lane
Scarsdale, NY 10583
Anthony Arenella,
Director
(914) 725-5500

SCHOOL WITHOUT WALLS
480 Broadway
Rochester, NY 14607

Dan Drmacich, Program
Administrator
(716) 546-6732

UNIVERSITY HEIGHTS HIGH
SCHOOL
University Avenue & West
181st Street
New York, NY 10453
Nancy Mohr, Principal
(212) 220-6397

PENNSYLVANIA
ALTERNATIVE FOR THE
MIDDLE YEARS
Washington and
Musgrave Streets
Philadelphia, PA 19144
Holly H. Perry,
Principal
Ted Toluba, Coordinator
(215) 843-4848

THE CREFELD SCHOOL
8836 Crefeld Street
Philadelphia, PA 19118
Charles Como,
Headmaster

Michael Patron,
Coordinator
(215) 242-5545

ELIZABETHTOWN AREA
HIGH SCHOOL
600 East High Street
Elizabethtown, PA 17022
Dustin Peters, Principal
(717) 367-1521

RHODE ISLAND
GORDON SCHOOL
Maxfield Avenue
East Providence, RI 09214
Darcey Hall, Principal
Joann Watson,
Coordinator
(401) 434-3833

HOPE HIGH SCHOOL
324 Hope Street
Providence, RI 02906
Paul Gounaris, Principal
Albin Moser, Head
Teacher
(401) 456-9329

SCHOOL ONE
75 John Street
Providence, RI 02906

Bill O'Hearn, Principal
Bev Vileno, Coordinator
(401) 331-2497

ST. XAVIER ACADEMY
225 MacArthur Boulevard
Coventry, RI 02816
Kathy Siok, Principal
Joyce Blum,
Coordinator
(401) 826-2130

SOUTH CAROLINA
HEATHWOOD HALL
3000 South Beltline
Boulevard
Columbia, SC 29201
J. Robert Shirley,
Headmaster
Lark Palma, Dean of
Faculty
(803) 765-2309

TENNESSEE
HIXSON HIGH SCHOOL
5705 Middle Valley Pike
Chattanooga, TN 37343
Tom McCullough,
Principal

Cheri Dedmon,
Coordinator
(615) 842-4141

ST. ANDREWS—SEWANEE
St. Andrews, TN 37372
Rev. William S. Wade,
Headmaster
Sofia Wentz, Dean of
Faculty
(615) 598-5950

TEXAS
PASCHAL HIGH SCHOOL
3001 Forest Park
Boulevard
Fort Worth, TX 76110
Radford Gregg,
Principal
Larry Barnes,
Coordinator
(817) 926-5463

THE JUDSON MONTESSORI
SCHOOL
705 Trafalgar
San Antonio, TX 78216
Jim Judson, Director
(512) 344-3117

WESTBURY HIGH SCHOOL
5575 Gasmer Road
Houston, TX 77035
Dr. Shirley Johnson,
Principal
Karen Owen,
Coordinator
(713) 723-6015

VERMONT
THE PUTNEY SCHOOL
Elm Lea Farm
Putney, VT 05316
Gunther Brandt,
Director
(802) 387-5566

THE STOWE SCHOOL
Mountain Road
Stowe, VT 05672
David Gibson,
Headmaster
(802) 253-4861

WASHINGTON
FINN HILL JUNIOR HIGH
SCHOOL
8040 NE 132nd
Kirkland, WA 98034

Robert Strode, Principal
Bryce Nelson,
   Coordinator
(206) 821-6544

MERIDIAN JUNIOR HIGH
   SCHOOL
23480 120th Avenue, SE
Kent, WA 98031
   Michael Davidson,
      Principal
   Sally Haber,
      Coordinator
(206) 859-7383

WISCONSIN
LINCOLN HIGH SCHOOL
1433 South 8th Street
Manitowoc, WI 54220
   Douglas Molzahn,
      Principal

Roger Alexander,
   Chairman
(414) 683-4830

WALDEN III
1012 Center Street
Racine, WI 53403
   Charles Kent, Principal
(414) 631-7000

INTERNATIONAL

CANADA
BISHOP CARROLL HIGH
   SCHOOL
4624 Richard Road, SW
Calgary, Alberta T3E, 6L1
   Bernard Bajnok,
      Principal
   Doretta Mario, Co-
      Coordinator
   Ed Marchand, Co-
      Coordinator
(403) 249-6601

COUNCIL OF CHIEF STATE SCHOOL OFFICERS

ALABAMA
Dr. Wayne Teague
Superintendent of
   Education
State Department of
   Education
Gordon Persons Office
   Building
50 North Ripley Street
Montgomery, AL 36130-
   3901
(205) 242-9700

ALASKA
Mr. Steve Hole
Acting Commissioner of
   Education
State Department of
   Education
Alaska State Office
   Building
Pouch F
Juneau, AK 99811
(907) 465-2800

AMERICAN SAMOA
Mr. Lealofi Uiagalelei
Director of Education
Department of Education
Pago Pago, AS 96799
(OS) 633-5159

ARIZONA
Ms. C. Diane Bishop
Superintendent of Public
   Instruction
State Department of
   Education
1535 West Jefferson
Phoenix, AZ 85007
(602) 542-5156

ARKANSAS
Dr. Burton Elliott
Director, General
   Education Division
State Department of
   Education
Little Rock, AR 72201-1071
(501) 682-4204

CALIFORNIA
Mr. Bill Honig
Superintendent of Public
 Instruction
State Department of
 Education
721 Capitol Mall
Sacramento, CA 95814
(916) 445-4338

COLORADO
Dr. William T. Randall
Commissioner of
 Education
State Department of
 Education
201 East Colfax
Denver, CO 80203-1705
(303) 866-6806

CONNECTICUT
Mr. Gerald N. Tirozzi
Commissioner of
 Education
State Department of
 Education
165 Capitol Avenue
Room 308, State Office
 Building
Hartford, CT 06106
(203) 566-5061

DELAWARE
Dr. James L. Spartz
(Interim) Superintendent
 of Public Instruction
State Department of
 Public Instruction
Townsend Building, #279
Post Office Box 1402
Dover, DE 19903
(302) 739-4601

DEPARTMENT OF
 DEFENSE
 DEPENDENTS
 SCHOOLS
Dr. John Stremple
Director
Department of Defense
Office of Dependents
 Schools
2461 Eisenhower Avenue
Alexandria, VA 22331-1100
(703) 325-0188

DISTRICT OF COLUMBIA
Mr. William H. Brown
(Interim) Superintendent
 of Public Schools
District of Columbia
 Public Schools

415 12th Street, N.W.
Washington, DC 20004
(202) 724-4222

FLORIDA
Ms. Betty Castor
Commissioner of
    Education
State Department of
    Education
Capitol Building, Room
    PL 08
Tallahassee, FL 32399
(904) 487-1785

GEORGIA
Dr. Werner Rogers
Superintendent of Schools
State Department of
    Education
2066 Twin Towers East
205 Butler Street
Atlanta, GA 30334
(404) 656-2800

GUAM
Ms. Anita A. Sukola
Director of Education
Department of Education
Post Office Box DE

Agana, GM 96910
(OS) 671-477-4978

HAWAII
Mr. Charles Toguchi
Superintendent of
    Education
Department of Education
Post Office Box 2360
1390 Miller Street, #307
Honolulu, HI 96804
(808) 586-3310

IDAHO
Mr. Jerry L. Evans
Superintendent of Public
    Instruction
State Department of
    Education
650 West State Street
Boise, ID 83720
(208) 334-3300

ILLINOIS
Mr. Robert Leininger
Superintendent of
    Education
State Board of Education
100 North First Street
Springfield, IL 62777
(217) 782-2221

INDIANA
Dr. H. Dean Evans
Superintendent of Public
 Instruction
State Department of
 Education
State House, Room 229
Indianapolis, IN 46204-
 2798
(317) 232-6665

IOWA
Dr. William L. Lepley
Director of Education
State Department of
 Education
Grimes State Office
 Building
East 14th & Grand Streets
Des Moines, IA 50319-
 0146
(515) 281-5294

KANSAS
Dr. Lee Droegemueller
Commissioner of
 Education
State Department of
 Education
120 East Tenth Street

Topeka, KS 66612
(913) 296-3202

KENTUCKY
Dr. Thomas C. Boysen
Superintendent of Public
 Instruction
State Department of
 Education
1725 Capitol Plaza Tower
Frankfort, KY 40601
(502) 564-4770

LOUISIANA
Dr. Wilmer S. Cody
Superintendent of
 Education
State Department of
 Education
Post Office Box 94064
Baton Rouge, LA 70804-
 9064
(504) 342-3602

MAINE
Dr. Eve M. Bither
Commissioner of
 Education
Maine Department of
 Education

State House, Station #23
Augusta, ME 04333
(207) 289-5800

MARYLAND
Dr. Joseph L. Shilling
State Superintendent of
   Schools
State Department of
   Education
200 West Baltimore Street
Baltimore, MD 21201
(301) 333-2200

MASSACHUSETTS
Mr. Harold Raynolds, Jr.
Commissioner of
   Education
State Department of
   Education
Quincy Center Plaza
1385 Hancock Street
Quincy, MA 02169
(617) 770-7300

MICHIGAN
Mr. Donald L. Bemis
Superintendent of Public
   Instruction

State Department of
   Education
Post Office Box 30008
608 West Allegan Street
Lansing, MI 48909
(517) 373-3354

MINNESOTA
Mr. Thomas A. Nelson
Commissioner of
   Education
State Department of
   Education
712 Capitol Square
   Building
550 Cedar Street
St. Paul, MN 55101
(612) 296-2358

MISSISSIPPI
Dr. Richard Thompson
Superintendent of
   Education
State Department of
   Education
P.O. Box 771, High Street
Jackson, MS 39205-0771
(601) 359-3513

MISSOURI
Dr. Robert E. Bartman
Commissioner of
 Education
Department of
 Elementary &
 Secondary
 Education
Post Office Box 480
205 Jefferson Street, 6th
 Floor
Jefferson City, MO 65102
(314) 751-4446

MONTANA
Ms. Nancy Keenan
Superintendent of Public
 Instruction
State Office of Public
 Instruction
106 State Capitol
Helena, MT 59620
(406) 444-3680

NEBRASKA
Dr. Joseph E. Lutjeharms
Commissioner of
 Education
State Department of
 Education

Post Office Box 94987
301 Centennial Mall,
 South
Lincoln, NE 68509
(402) 471-2465

NEVADA
Dr. Eugene T. Paslov
Superintendent of Public
 Instruction
State Department of
 Education
400 West King Street
Capitol Complex
Carson City, NV 89710
(702) 885-3100

NEW HAMPSHIRE
Dr. Charles H. Marston
Commissioner of
 Education
State Department of
 Education
101 Pleasant Street
State Office Park South
Concord, NH 03301
(603) 271-3144

123

NEW JERSEY
Mr. John Ellis
Commissioner of
 Education
State Department of
 Education
225 West State Street
Trenton, NJ 08625-0500
(609) 292-4450

NEW MEXICO
Mr. Alan Morgan
Superintendent of Public
 Instruction
State Department of
 Education
State Dept of Education
 Building
300 Don Gaspar
Santa Fe, NM 87501-2786
(505) 827-6516

NEW YORK
Dr. Thomas Sobol
Commissioner of
 Education
State Education
 Department
111 Education Building

Washington Avenue
Albany, NY 12234
(518) 474-5844

NORTH CAROLINA
Mr. Bob R. Etheridge
Superintendent of Public
 Instruction
State Department of
 Public Instruction
Education Building, Room
 318
Edenton & Salisbury
 Streets
Raleigh, NC 27603-1712
(919) 733-3813

NORTH DAKOTA
Dr. Wayne G. Sanstead
Superintendent of Public
 Instruction
State Department of
 Public Instruction
State Capitol Building,
 11th Floor
600 Boulevard Avenue
 East
Bismarck, ND 58505-0164
(701) 224-2261

NORTHERN MARIANA ISLANDS
Ms. Elizabeth Diaz Rechebei
Commissioner of Education
Commonwealth of the Northern Mariana Islands
Department of Education
P.O. Box 1370 CK
Saipan, CM 96950
(OS) 322-0311

OHIO
Dr. Franklin B. Walter
Superintendent of Public Instruction
State Department of Education
65 South Front Street, Room 808
Columbus, OH 43266-0308
(614) 466-3304

OKLAHOMA
Ms. Sandy Garrett
Superintendent of Public Instruction
State Department of Education
Oliver Hodge Memorial Education Building
2500 North Lincoln Boulevard
Oklahoma City, OK 73105-4599
(405) 521-3301

OREGON
Ms. Norma Paulus
Superintendent of Public Instruction
State Department of Education
700 Pringle Parkway, S.E.
Salem, OR 97310
(503) 378-3573

PENNSYLVANIA
Mr. Donald M. Carroll Jr.
Secretary of Education
State Department of Education
333 Market Street, 10th Floor
Harrisburg, PA 17126
(717) 787-5820

PUERTO RICO
Mr. Jose Lema Moya
Secretary of Education
Department of Education
Post Office Box 759
Hato Rey, PR 00919
(809) 751-5372

RHODE ISLAND
Dr. J. Troy Earhart
Commissioner of
    Education
State Department of
    Education
22 Hayes Street
Providence, RI 02908
(401) 277-2031

SOUTH CAROLINA
Dr. Barbara S. Neilsen
State Superintendent of
    Education
State Department of
    Education
1006 Rutledge Building
1429 Senate Street
Columbia, SC 29201
(803) 734-8492

SOUTH DAKOTA
Dr. Henry Kosters
State Superintendent
Department of Education
    & Cultural Affairs
Division of Elementary &
    Secondary Education
700 Governors Drive
Pierre, SD 57501
(605) 773-3243

TENNESSEE
Dr. Charles E. Smith
Commissioner of
    Education
State Department of
    Education
100 Cordell Hull Building
Nashville, TN 37219
(615) 741-2731

TEXAS
Dr. William N. Kirby
Commissioner of
    Education
Texas Education Agency
William B. Travis Building
1701 North Congress
    Avenue
Austin, TX 78701-1494
(512) 463-8985

UTAH
Mr. Jay B. Taggart
Superintendent of Public
    Instruction
State Office of Education
250 East 500 South
Salt Lake City, UT 84111
(801) 538-7510

VERMONT
Mr. Richard P. Mills
Commissioner of
    Education
State Department of
    Education
120 State Street
Montpelier, VT 05602-
    2703
(802) 828-3135

VIRGIN ISLANDS
Dr. Linda Creque
Commissioner of
    Education
Department of Education
44–46 Kogens Gade
St. Thomas, VI 00802
(809) 774-2810

VIRGINIA
Dr. Joseph A. Spagnolo Jr.
Superintendent of Public
    Instruction
State Department of
    Education
P.O. Box 6Q
James Monroe Building
Fourteenth & Franklin
    Streets
Richmond, VA 23216-2060
(804) 225-2023

WASHINGTON
Ms. Judith A. Billings
Superintendent of Public
    Instruction
State Department of
    Public Instruction
Old Capitol Building
Washington & Legion
Mail Stop FG-11
Olympia, WA 98504
(206) 586-6904

WEST VIRGINIA
Mr. Henry Marockie
State Superintendent of
    Schools

State Department of
 Education
1900 Washington Street
Building B, Room 358
Charleston, WV 25305
(304) 348-2681

WISCONSIN
Dr. Herbert J. Grover
Superintendent of Public
 Instruction
State Department of
 Public Instruction
125 South Webster Street
Post Office Box 7841
Madison, WI 53707
(608) 266-1771

WYOMING
Ms. Diana Ohman
State Superintendent of
 Public Instruction

State Department of
 Education
Hathaway Building
Cheyenne, WY 82002
(307) 777-7675

COUNCIL OF CHIEF
 STATE
SCHOOL OFFICERS
Mr. Gordon M. Ambach
Executive Director
Council of Chief State
 School Officers
379 Hall of the States
400 North Capitol Street,
 NW
Washington, DC 20001
(202) 393-8161

TEACHERS' COLLEGES

As institutional members of The Holmes Group, nearly 100 schools of education have committed themselves to elevating and evolving the preparation of our teachers so that they can improve the education of today's children.

These are the member schools of The Holmes Group. Give them your support.

Alabama, University of
Alaska, University of
Arizona State University
Arkansas, University of
Auburn University
Bank Street College of Education
Baylor University
California-Berkeley, Univ. of
California-Davis, Univ. of
Catholic University of America
Chicago, University of
Cincinnati, University of
Clark University
Colorado, University of
Colorado State University
Connecticut, University of
Delaware, University of
Duke University
Emory University
Fordham University
George Mason University
Georgia State University
Hampton University
Harvard University

Hawaii, University of
Houston, University of
Howard University
Idaho, University of
Illinois-Chicago, Univ. of
Illinois-Urbana/Champaign, Univ. of
Iowa, University of
Iowa State University
Kansas, University of
Kansas State University
Kent State University
Kentucky, University of
Lehigh University
Louisiana State University
Maine, University of
Maryland, University of
Massachusetts-Amherst, Univ. of
Michigan, University of
Michigan State University
Minnesota, University of
Mississippi, University of
Mississippi State University
Missouri-Columbia, Univ. of

Missouri-Kansas City, Univ. of
Missouri-St. Louis, Univ. of
Nebraska, University of
Nevada, University of
New Hampshire, University of
New Mexico, University of
New Mexico State University
New York University
North Carolina AT&T
North Carolina-Chapel Hill,
   Univ. of
North Dakota, University of
Ohio, University of
Ohio State University
Oklahoma, University of
Oklahoma State University
Oregon, University of
Oregon State University
Pennsylvania, University of
Pittsburgh, University of
Prairie View A&M University
Purdue University
Rhode Island, University of
Rochester, University of
Rutgers University
South Carolina, University of

South Dakota, University of
South Florida, University of
Southern California, Univ. of
Stanford University
SUNY-Albany
SUNY-Buffalo
Syracuse University
Teachers College, Columbia,
   Univ. of
Temple University
Tennessee, University of
Texas A&M University
Texas Tech University
Texas-Austin, University of
Trinity University
Utah, University of
Vermont, University of
Virginia, University of
Virginia Commonwealth Univ.
Virginia Polytechnic & State Univ.
Washington, University of
Wayne State University
West Virginia University
Wisconsin-Madison, Univ. of
Wisconsin-Milwaukee, Univ. of
Wyoming, University of

HEAD START
DEPARTMENT OF HEALTH & HUMAN SERVICES

NATIONAL HEADQUARTERS

Commissioner
Administration for Children, Youth & Family
U.S. Department of Health & Human Services
P.O. Box 1182, Washington, DC 20013

REGIONAL OFFICES

REGION I

Office of Human Development Services
Department of Health & Human Services
Room 2000 Federal Building
Government Center
Boston, Massachusetts 02203
(617) 565-1139
(Connecticut, Maine, Massachusetts, New Hampshire,
    Vermont, Rhode Island)

REGION II

Office of Human Development Services
Department of Health & Human Services
Room 4149 Federal Building
26 Federal Plaza
New York, New York 10278
(212) 264-2974
(New York, New Jersey, Puerto Rico, Virgin Islands)

REGION III

Office of Human Development Services
Department of Health & Human Services
3535 Market Street
P.O. Box 13716
Philadelphia, Pennsylvania 19101
(215) 596-1224
(Delaware, Washington, D.C., Maryland, Pennsylvania,
   Virginia, West Virginia)

REGION IV

Office of Human Development Services
Department of Health & Human Services
101 Marietta Tower, Suite 903
Atlanta, Georgia 30323
(404) 331-2034
(Alabama, Florida, Georgia, Kentucky, Mississippi, North
   Carolina, South Carolina, Tennessee)

REGION V

Office of Human Development Services
Department of Health & Human Services
105 West Adams Street, 21st Floor
Chicago, Illinois 60603
(312) 353-4241
(Illinois, Indiana, Michigan, Minnesota, Ohio, Wisconsin)

REGION VI

Office of Human Development Services
Department of Health & Human Services
1200 Main Tower Building
Dallas, Texas 75202
(214) 767-2981
(Arkansas, Louisiana, New Mexico, Oklahoma, Texas)

REGION VII

Office of Human Development Services
Department of Health & Human Services
601 E. 12th Street
Room 384 Federal Building
Kansas City, Missouri 64106
(816) 426-5401
(Iowa, Kansas, Missouri, Nebraska)

REGION VIII

Office of Human Development Services
Department of Health & Human Services
1961 Stout Street, Room 1194
Denver, Colorado 80294
(303) 844-2622
(Colorado, Montana, North Dakota, Utah, Wyoming,
   South Dakota)

REGION IX

Office of Human Development Services
Department of Health & Human Services
50 United Nations Plaza, Room 450
San Francisco, California 94102
(415) 556-6153
(Arizona, California, Hawaii, Nevada, Pacific Trust
  Territories)

REGION X

Office of Human Development Services
Department of Health & Human Services
Blanchard Plaza
2201 Sixth Ave., RX 32
Seattle, Washington 98121
(206) 442-0838
(Alaska, Idaho, Oregon, Washington)

AMERICAN INDIAN PROGRAM BRANCH

Head Start Bureau
Department of Health & Human Services
P.O. Box 1182
Washington, D.C. 20013
(202) 245-0436

MIGRANT PROGRAM BRANCH

Head Start Bureau
Department of Health & Human Services
P.O. Box 1182
Washington, D.C. 20013
(202) 245-0455